D F ||||| ||| | |||||| ||| |||| |||
W9-AYV-600

Doug —

With gratitude, as ever,
for your welcome at
Colby, and for being a
"hearer and heartener of the work"

Seamus
25·ii·'93

BOOKS BY SEAMUS HEANEY

POETRY
Death of a Naturalist
Door into the Dark
Wintering Out
North
Field Work
Poems 1965–1975
Sweeney Astray: A Version from the Irish
Station Island
The Haw Lantern
Selected Poems 1966–1987

CRITICISM
Preoccupations
The Government of the Tongue

Selected Poems 1966–1987

Seamus Heaney

Selected Poems

1966–1987

Farrar, Straus and Giroux

New York

Copyright © 1990 by Seamus Heaney
All rights reserved
Library of Congress catalog card number: 90-81169
Printed in the United States of America
Designed by Cynthia Krupat
First published in 1990 by Faber and Faber Limited
First American edition, 1990

For Marie and Michael

and Christopher and Catherine Ann

Contents

FROM

Stations

(1 9 7 5)

FROM

North

(1 9 7 5)

FROM

Field Work

(1979)

cf   Act of Union
Bog poems

FROM

The Haw Lantern

(1987)

FROM

Death of a Naturalist

(1 9 6 6)

Digging

Kavovogy 4
sounds of place
Thocar

Between my finger and my thumb
The squat pen rests; snug as a gun.

Under my window, a clean rasping sound
When the spade sinks into gravelly ground:
My father, digging. I look down

Till his straining rump among the flowerbeds
Bends low, comes up twenty years away
Stooping in rhythm through potato drills
Where he was digging.

The coarse boot nestled on the lug, the shaft
Against the inside knee was levered firmly.
He rooted out tall tops, buried the bright edge deep
To scatter new potatoes that we picked
Loving their cool hardness in our hands.

By God, the old man could handle a spade.
Just like his old man.

My grandfather cut more turf in a day
Than any other man on Toner's bog.
Once I carried him milk in a bottle
Corked sloppily with paper. He straightened up
To drink it, then fell to right away
Nicking and slicing neatly, heaving sods
Over his shoulder, going down and down
For the good turf. Digging.

The cold smell of potato mould, the squelch and slap
Of soggy peat, the curt cuts of an edge
Through living roots awaken in my head.
But I've no spade to follow men like them.

Between my finger and my thumb
The squat pen rests.
I'll dig with it.

o~ ww ┌ magpies
┌ Preoccupations

Death of a Naturalist

All year the flax-dam festered in the heart
Of the townland; green and heavy-headed
Flax had rotted there, weighted down by huge sods.
Daily it sweltered in the punishing sun.
Bubbles gargled delicately, bluebottles
Wove a strong gauze of sound around the smell.
There were dragonflies, spotted butterflies,
But best of all was the warm thick slobber
Of frogspawn that grew like clotted water
In the shade of the banks. Here, every spring
I would fill jampotfuls of the jellied
Specks to range on window-sills at home,
On shelves at school, and wait and watch until
The fattening dots burst into nimble-
Swimming tadpoles. Miss Walls would tell us how
The daddy frog was called a bullfrog
And how he croaked and how the mammy frog
Laid hundreds of little eggs and this was
Frogspawn. You could tell the weather by frogs too
For they were yellow in the sun and brown
In rain.

    Then one hot day when fields were rank
With cowdung in the grass the angry frogs
Invaded the flax-dam; I ducked through hedges
To a coarse croaking that I had not heard
Before. The air was thick with a bass chorus.
Right down the dam gross-bellied frogs were cocked
On sods; their loose necks pulsed like sails. Some hopped:

The slap and plop were obscene threats. Some sat
Poised like mud grenades, their blunt heads farting.
I sickened, turned, and ran. The great slime kings
Were gathered there for vengeance and I knew
That if I dipped my hand the spawn would clutch it.

Blackberry-Picking

For Philip Hobsbaum

Late August, given heavy rain and sun
For a full week, the blackberries would ripen.
At first, just one, a glossy purple clot
Among others, red, green, hard as a knot.
You ate that first one and its flesh was sweet
Like thickened wine: summer's blood was in it
Leaving stains upon the tongue and lust for
Picking. Then red ones inked up and that hunger
Sent us out with milk cans, pea tins, jam pots
Where briars scratched and wet grass bleached our boots.
Round hayfields, cornfields and potato drills
We trekked and picked until the cans were full,
Until the tinkling bottom had been covered
With green ones, and on top big dark blobs burned
Like a plate of eyes. Our hands were peppered
With thorn pricks, our palms sticky as Bluebeard's.

We hoarded the fresh berries in the byre.
But when the bath was filled we found a fur,
A rat-grey fungus, glutting on our cache.
The juice was stinking too. Once off the bush
The fruit fermented, the sweet flesh would turn sour.
I always felt like crying. It wasn't fair
That all the lovely canfuls smelt of rot.
Each year I hoped they'd keep, knew they would not.

Follower

My father worked with a horse-plough,
His shoulders globed like a full sail strung
Between the shafts and the furrow.
The horses strained at his clicking tongue.

An expert. He would set the wing
And fit the bright steel-pointed sock.
The sod rolled over without breaking.
At the headrig, with a single pluck

Of reins, the sweating team turned round
And back into the land. His eye
Narrowed and angled at the ground,
Mapping the furrow exactly.

I stumbled in his hobnailed wake,
Fell sometimes on the polished sod;
Sometimes he rode me on his back
Dipping and rising to his plod.

I wanted to grow up and plough,
To close one eye, stiffen my arm.
All I ever did was follow
In his broad shadow round the farm.

I was a nuisance, tripping, falling,
Yapping always. But today
It is my father who keeps stumbling
Behind me, and will not go away.

Mid-Term Break

I sat all morning in the college sick bay
Counting bells knelling classes to a close.
At two o'clock our neighbours drove me home.

In the porch I met my father crying—
He had always taken funerals in his stride—
And Big Jim Evans saying it was a hard blow.

The baby cooed and laughed and rocked the pram
When I came in, and I was embarrassed
By old men standing up to shake my hand

And tell me they were 'sorry for my trouble'.
Whispers informed strangers I was the eldest,
Away at school, as my mother held my hand

In hers and coughed out angry tearless sighs.
At ten o'clock the ambulance arrived
With the corpse, stanched and bandaged by the nurses.

Next morning I went up into the room. Snowdrops
And candles soothed the bedside; I saw him
For the first time in six weeks. Paler now,

Wearing a poppy bruise on his left temple,
He lay in the four-foot box as in his cot.
No gaudy scars, the bumper knocked him clear.

A four-foot box, a foot for every year.

Poem

For Marie

Love, I shall perfect for you the child
Who diligently potters in my brain
Digging with heavy spade till sods were piled
Or puddling through muck in a deep drain.

Yearly I would sow my yard-long garden.
I'd strip a layer of sods to build the wall
That was to keep out sow and pecking hen.
Yearly, admitting these, the sods would fall.

Or in the sucking clabber I would splash
Delightedly and dam the flowing drain
But always my bastions of clay and mush
Would burst before the rising autumn rain.

Love, you shall perfect for me this child
Whose small imperfect limits would keep breaking:
Within new limits now, arrange the world
And square the circle: four walls and a ring.

Personal Helicon

For Michael Longley

As a child, they could not keep me from wells
And old pumps with buckets and windlasses.
I loved the dark drop, the trapped sky, the smells
Of waterweed, fungus and dank moss.

One, in a brickyard, with a rotted board top.
I savoured the rich crash when a bucket
Plummeted down at the end of a rope.
So deep you saw no reflection in it.

A shallow one under a dry stone ditch
Fructified like any aquarium.
When you dragged out long roots from the soft mulch
A white face hovered over the bottom.

Others had echoes, gave back your own call
With a clean new music in it. And one
Was scaresome, for there, out of ferns and tall
Foxgloves, a rat slapped across my reflection.

Now, to pry into roots, to finger slime,
To stare, big-eyed Narcissus, into some spring
Is beneath all adult dignity. I rhyme
To see myself, to set the darkness echoing.

FROM

Door into the Dark

(1 9 6 9)

Thatcher

Bespoke for weeks, he turned up some morning
Unexpectedly, his bicycle slung
With a light ladder and a bag of knives.
He eyed the old rigging, poked at the eaves,

Opened and handled sheaves of lashed wheat-straw.
Next, the bundled rods: hazel and willow
Were flicked for weight, twisted in case they'd snap.
It seemed he spent the morning warming up:

Then fixed the ladder, laid out well-honed blades
And snipped at straw and sharpened ends of rods
That, bent in two, made a white-pronged staple
For pinning down his world, handful by handful.

Couchant for days on sods above the rafters,
He shaved and flushed the butts, stitched all together
Into a sloped honeycomb, a stubble patch,
And left them gaping at his Midas touch.

The Peninsula

When you have nothing more to say, just drive
For a day all round the peninsula.
The sky is tall as over a runway,
The land without marks so you will not arrive

But pass through, though always skirting landfall.
At dusk, horizons drink down sea and hill,
The ploughed field swallows the whitewashed gable
And you're in the dark again. Now recall

The glazed foreshore and silhouetted log,
That rock where breakers shredded into rags,
The leggy birds stilted on their own legs,
Islands riding themselves out into the fog

And drive back home, still with nothing to say
Except that now you will uncode all landscapes
By this: things founded clean on their own shapes,
Water and ground in their extremity.

see Interview

Requiem for the Croppies

The pockets of our greatcoats full of barley—
No kitchens on the run, no striking camp—
We moved quick and sudden in our own country.
The priest lay behind ditches with the tramp.
A people, hardly marching—on the hike—
We found new tactics happening each day:
We'd cut through reins and rider with the pike
And stampede cattle into infantry,
Then retreat through hedges where cavalry must be thrown.
Until, on Vinegar Hill, the fatal conclave.
Terraced thousands died, shaking scythes at cannon.
The hillside blushed, soaked in our broken wave.
They buried us without shroud or coffin
And in August the barley grew up out of the grave.

1) What do you see?
cf.   Glory   1166 [1916]

2) Political?

Interview

The Wife's Tale

When I had spread it all on linen cloth
Under the hedge, I called them over.
The hum and gulp of the thresher ran down
And the big belt slewed to a standstill, straw
Hanging undelivered in the jaws.
There was such quiet that I heard their boots
Crunching the stubble twenty yards away.

He lay down and said 'Give these fellows theirs,
I'm in no hurry,' plucking grass in handfuls
And tossing it in the air. 'That looks well.'
(He nodded at my white cloth on the grass.)
'I declare a woman could lay out a field
Though boys like us have little call for cloths.'
He winked, then watched me as I poured a cup
And buttered the thick slices that he likes.
'It's threshing better than I thought, and mind
It's good clean seed. Away over there and look.'
Always this inspection has to be made
Even when I don't know what to look for.

But I ran my hand in the half-filled bags
Hooked to the slots. It was hard as shot,
Innumerable and cool. The bags gaped
Where the chutes ran back to the stilled drum
And forks were stuck at angles in the ground
As javelins might mark lost battlefields.
I moved between them back across the stubble.

They lay in the ring of their own crusts and dregs
Smoking and saying nothing. 'There's good yield,
Isn't there?'—as proud as if he were the land itself—
'Enough for crushing and for sowing both.'
And that was it. I'd come and he had shown me,
So I belonged no further to the work.
I gathered cups and folded up the cloth
And went. But they still kept their ease
Spread out, unbuttoned, grateful, under the trees.

Night Drive

word ?

The smells of ordinariness
Were new on the night drive through France:
Rain and hay and woods on the air
Made warm draughts in the open car.

Signposts whitened relentlessly.
Montreuil, Abbéville, Beauvais
Were promised, promised, came and went,
Each place granting its name's fulfilment.

A combine groaning its way late
Bled seeds across its work-light.
A forest fire smouldered out.
One by one small cafés shut.

I thought of you continuously
A thousand miles south where Italy
Laid its loin to France on the darkened sphere.
Your ordinariness was renewed there.

Relic of Memory

The lough waters
Can petrify wood:
Old oars and posts
Over the years
Harden their grain,
Incarcerate ghosts

Of sap and season.
The shallows lap
And give and take:
Constant ablutions,
Such drowning love
Stun a stake

To stalagmite.
Dead lava,
The cooling star,
Coal and diamond
Or sudden birth
Of burnt meteor

Are too simple,
Without the lure
That relic stored—
A piece of stone
On the shelf at school,
Oatmeal-coloured.

Bogland

Berkeley 1970-71
(also C.C. O'Brien)

For T. P. Flanagan

We have no prairies
To slice a big sun at evening—
Everywhere the eye concedes to
Encroaching horizon,

Is wooed into the cyclops' eye
Of a tarn. Our unfenced country
Is bog that keeps crusting
Between the sights of the sun.

They've taken the skeleton
Of the Great Irish Elk
Out of the peat, set it up,
An astounding crate full of air.

Butter sunk under
More than a hundred years
Was recovered salty and white.
The ground itself is kind, black butter

Melting and opening underfoot,
Missing its last definition
By millions of years.
They'll never dig coal here,

Only the waterlogged trunks
Of great firs, soft as pulp.
Our pioneers keep striking
Inwards and downwards,

Every layer they strip
Seems camped on before.
The bogholes might be Atlantic seepage.
The wet centre is bottomless.

FROM

Wintering Out

———————————

(1 9 7 2)

Bog Oak

A carter's trophy
split for rafters,
a cobwebbed, black,
long-seasoned rib

under the first thatch.
I might tarry
with the moustached
dead, the creel-fillers,

or eavesdrop on
their hopeless wisdom
as a blow-down of smoke
struggles over the half-door

and mizzling rain
blurs the far end
of the cart track.
The softening ruts

lead back to no
'oak groves', no
cutters of mistletoe
in the green clearings.

Perhaps I just make out
Edmund Spenser,
dreaming sunlight,
encroached upon by

geniuses who creep
'out of every corner
of the woodes and glennes'
towards watercress and carrion.

Anahorish

My 'place of clear water',
the first hill in the world
where springs washed into
the shiny grass

and darkened cobbles
in the bed of the lane.
Anahorish, soft gradient
of consonant, vowel-meadow,

after-image of lamps
swung through the yards
on winter evenings.
With pails and barrows

those mound-dwellers
go waist-deep in mist
to break the light ice
at wells and dunghills.

Gifts of Rain

I

Cloudburst and steady downpour now
for days.
          Still mammal,
straw-footed on the mud,
he begins to sense weather
by his skin.

A nimble snout of flood
licks over stepping stones
and goes uprooting.
                    He fords
his life by sounding.
                    Soundings.

II

A man wading lost fields
breaks the pane of flood:

a flower of mud-
water blooms up to his reflection

like a cut swaying
its red spoors through a basin.

His hands grub
where the spade has uncastled

sunken drills, an atlantis
he depends on. So

he is hooped to where he planted
and sky and ground

are running naturally among his arms
that grope the cropping land.

III

When rains were gathering
there would be an all-night
roaring off the ford.
Their world-schooled ear

could monitor the usual
confabulations, the race
slabbering past the gable,
the Moyola harping on

its gravel beds:
all spouts by daylight
brimmed with their own airs
and overflowed each barrel

in long tresses.
I cock my ear
at an absence—
in the shared calling of blood

arrives my need
for antediluvian lore.

Soft voices of the dead
are whispering by the shore

that I would question
(and for my children's sake)
about crops rotted, river mud
glazing the baked clay floor.

IV

The tawny guttural water
spells itself: Moyola
is its own score and consort,

bedding the locale
in the utterance,
reed music, an old chanter

breathing its mists
through vowels and history.
A swollen river,

a mating call of sound   *Rich mo. n Colte*
rises to pleasure me, Dives,
hoarder of common ground.

Broagh

Riverbank, the long rigs
ending in broad docken
and a canopied pad
down to the ford.

The garden mould
bruised easily, the shower
gathering in your heelmark
was the black *O*

in *Broagh*,
its low tattoo
among the windy boortrees
and rhubarb-blades

ended almost
suddenly, like that last
gh the strangers found
difficult to manage.

Oracle

Hide in the hollow trunk
of the willow tree,
its listening familiar,
until, as usual, they
cuckoo your name
across the fields.
You can hear them
draw the poles of stiles
as they approach
calling you out:
small mouth and ear
in a woody cleft,
lobe and larynx
of the mossy places.

A New Song

I met a girl from Derrygarve
And the name, a lost potent musk,
Recalled the river's long swerve,
A kingfisher's blue bolt at dusk

And stepping stones like black molars
Sunk in the ford, the shifty glaze
Of the whirlpool, the Moyola
Pleasuring beneath alder trees.

And Derrygarve, I thought, was just:
Vanished music, twilit water—
A smooth libation of the past
Poured by this chance vestal daughter.

But now our river tongues must rise
From licking deep in native haunts
To flood, with vowelling embrace,
Demesnes staked out in consonants.

And Castledawson we'll enlist
And Upperlands, each planted bawn—
Like bleaching-greens resumed by grass—
A vocable, as rath and bullaun.

The Other Side

I

Thigh-deep in sedge and marigolds
a neighbour laid his shadow
on the stream, vouching

'It's poor as Lazarus, that ground,'
and brushed away
among the shaken leafage.

I lay where his lea sloped
to meet our fallow,
nested on moss and rushes,

my ear swallowing
his fabulous, biblical dismissal,
that tongue of chosen people.

When he would stand like that
on the other side, white-haired,
swinging his blackthorn

at the marsh weeds,
he prophesied above our scraggy acres,
then turned away

towards his promised furrows
on the hill, a wake of pollen
drifting to our bank, next season's tares.

vetches

36

II

For days we would rehearse
each patriarchal dictum:
Lazarus, the Pharaoh, Solomon

and David and Goliath rolled
magnificently, like loads of hay
too big for our small lanes,

or faltered on a rut—
'Your side of the house, I believe,
hardly rule by the Book at all.'

His brain was a whitewashed kitchen
hung with texts, swept tidy
as the body o' the kirk.

III

Then sometimes when the rosary was dragging
mournfully on in the kitchen
we would hear his step round the gable

though not until after the litany
would the knock come to the door
and the casual whistle strike up

on the doorstep. 'A right-looking night,'
he might say, 'I was dandering by
and says I, I might as well call.'

But now I stand behind him
in the dark yard, in the moan of prayers,
He puts a hand in a pocket

or taps a little tune with the blackthorn
shyly, as if he were party to
lovemaking or a stranger's weeping.

Should I slip away, I wonder,
or go up and touch his shoulder
and talk about the weather

or the price of grass-seed?

How was (This) rage shall heavenly hope ... befitting our glaus of adversity.

The Tollund Man

I

Some day I will go to Aarhus
To see his peat-brown head,
The mild pods of his eye-lids,
His pointed skin cap.

In the flat country nearby
Where they dug him out,
His last gruel of winter seeds
Caked in his stomach,

Naked except for
The cap, noose and girdle,
I will stand a long time.
Bridegroom to the goddess,

She tightened her torc on him
And opened her fen,
Those dark juices working
Him to a saint's kept body,

Trove of the turfcutters'
Honeycombed workings.
Now his stained face
Reposes at Aarhus.

II

I could risk blasphemy,
Consecrate the cauldron bog

situation (promise of pilgrimage)

Our holy ground and pray
Him to make germinate

The scattered, ambushed
Flesh of labourers,
Stockinged corpses
Laid out in the farmyards,

Tell-tale skin and teeth
Flecking the sleepers
Of four young brothers, trailed
For miles along the lines.

III

Something of his sad freedom
As he rode the tumbril
Should come to me, driving,
Saying the names

Tollund, Grauballe, Nebelgard,
Watching the pointing hands
Of country people,
Not knowing their tongue.

Out there in Jutland
In the old man-killing parishes
I will feel lost,
Unhappy and at home.

Originally Powell — personal poems

Wedding Day

I am afraid.
Sound has stopped in the day
And the images reel over
And over. Why all those tears,

The wild grief on his face
Outside the taxi? The sap
Of mourning rises
In our waving guests.

You sing behind the tall cake
Like a deserted bride
Who persists, demented,
And goes through the ritual.

When I went to the Gents
There was a skewered heart
And a legend of love. Let me
Sleep on your breast to the airport.

Summer Home

Was it wind off the dumps
or something in heat

dogging us, the summer gone sour,
a fouled nest incubating somewhere?

Whose fault, I wondered, inquisitor
of the possessed air.

To realize suddenly,
whip off the mat

that was larval, moving—
and scald, scald, scald.

Bushing the door, my arms full
of wild cherry and rhododendron,
I hear her small lost weeping
through the hall, that bells and hoarsens
on my name, my name.

O love, here is the blame.

The loosened flowers between us
gather in, compose
for a May altar of sorts.

These frank and falling blooms
soon taint to a sweet chrism.   *consecrated   oil*

Attend. Anoint the wound.

III

Oh, we tented our wound all right
under the homely sheet

and lay as if the cold flat of a blade
had winded us.

More and more I postulate
thick healings, like now

as you bend in the shower
water lives down the tilting stoups of your breasts.

IV

With a final
unmusical drive
long grains begin
to open and split

ahead and once more
we sap
the white, trodden
path to the heart.

V

My children weep out the hot foreign night.
We walk the floor, my foul mouth takes it out
On you and we lie stiff till dawn
Attends the pillow, and the maize, and vine

That holds its filling burden to the light.
Yesterday rocks sang when we tapped
Stalactites in the cave's old, dripping dark—
Our love calls tiny as a tuning fork.

Limbo

Fishermen at Ballyshannon
Netted an infant last night
Along with the salmon.
An illegitimate spawning,

A small one thrown back
To the waters. But I'm sure
As she stood in the shallows
Ducking him tenderly

Till the frozen knobs of her wrists
Were dead as the gravel,
He was a minnow with hooks
Tearing her open.

She waded in under
The sign of her cross.
He was hauled in with the fish.
Now limbo will be

A cold glitter of souls
Through some far briny zone.
Even Christ's palms, unhealed,
Smart and cannot fish there.

(1) gesture?
→ moral attitude
of poem?

(2) worker, inform

(3) limbo

(4) christ

Bye-Child

He was discovered in the henhouse
where she had confined him. He was
incapable of saying anything.

When the lamp glowed,
A yolk of light
In their back window,
The child in the outhouse
Put his eye to a chink—

Little henhouse boy,
Sharp-faced as new moons
Remembered, your photo still
Glimpsed like a rodent
On the floor of my mind,

Little moon man,
Kennelled and faithful
At the foot of the yard,
Your frail shape, luminous,
Weightless, is stirring the dust,

The cobwebs, old droppings
Under the roosts
And dry smells from scraps
She put through your trapdoor
Morning and evening.

After those footsteps, silence;
Vigils, solitudes, fasts,

Unchristened tears,
A puzzled love of the light.
But now you speak at last

With a remote mime
Of something beyond patience,
Your gaping wordless proof
Of lunar distances
Travelled beyond love.

Westering

In California

I sit under Rand McNally's
'Official Map of the Moon'—
The colour of frogskin,
Its enlarged pores held

Open and one called
'Pitiscus' at eye level—
Recalling the last night
In Donegal, my shadow

Neat upon the whitewash
From her bony shine,
The cobbles of the yard
Lit pale as eggs.

Summer had been a free fall
Ending there,
The empty amphitheatre
Of the west. Good Friday

We had started out
Past shopblinds drawn on the afternoon,
Cars stilled outside still churches,
Bikes tilting to a wall;

We drove by,
A dwindling interruption,
As clappers smacked
On a bare altar

And congregations bent
To the studded crucifix.
What nails dropped out that hour?
Roads unreeled, unreeled

Falling light as casts
Laid down
On shining waters.
Under the moon's stigmata

Six thousand miles away,
I imagine untroubled dust,
A loosening gravity,
Christ weighing by his hands.

Stations

(1 9 7 5)

Statvous ?
_____

OF   ie   cross — Crossing"
                          N + S
Morbings   Ulster — Republic
negotiations   Prot - RC

Nesting-Ground

The sandmartins' nests were loopholes of darkness in the riverbank. He could imagine his arm going in to the armpit, sleeved and straitened, but because he once felt the cold prick of a dead robin's claw and the surprising density of its tiny beak he only gazed.

He heard cheeping far in but because the men had once shown him a rat's nest in the butt of a stack where chaff and powdered cornstalks adhered to the moist pink necks and backs he only listened.

As he stood sentry, gazing, waiting, he thought of putting his ear to one of the abandoned holes and listening for the silence under the ground.

Nature [Fear] - articulivevess

53

England's Difficulty

I moved like a double agent among the big concepts.

The word 'enemy' had the toothed efficiency of a mowing machine. It was a mechanical and distant noise beyond that opaque security, that autonomous ignorance.

'When the Germans bombed Belfast it was the bitterest Orange parts were hit the worst.'

I was on somebody's shoulder, conveyed through the starlit yard to see the sky glowing over Anahorish. Grown-ups lowered their voices and resettled in the kitchen as if tired out after an excursion.

Behind the blackout, Germany called to lamplit kitchens through fretted baize, dry battery, wet battery, capillary wires, domed valves that squeaked and burbled as the dial-hand absolved Stuttgart and Leipzig.

'He's an artist, this Haw Haw. He can fairly leave it into them.'

I lodged with 'the enemies of Ulster', the scullions outside the walls. An adept at banter, I crossed the lines with carefully enunciated passwords, manned every speech with checkpoints and reported back to nobody.

54

Visitant

It kept treading air, as if it were a ghost with claims on us, precipitating in the heat tremor. Then, released from its distorting mirror, up the fields there comes this awkwardly smiling foreigner, awkwardly received, who gentled the long Sunday afternoon just by sitting with us.

Where are you now, real visitant, who vivified 'parole' and 'POW'? Where are the rings garnetted with bits of toothbrush, the ships in bottles, the Tyrol landscapes globed in electric bulbs?

'They've hands for anything, these Germans.'

He walked back into the refining lick of the grass, behind the particular judgements of captor and harbourer. As he walks yet, feeling our eyes on his back, treading the air of the image he achieved, released to his fatigues.

Trial Runs

WELCOME HOME YE LADS OF THE EIGHTH ARMY. There must be some defiance in it because it was painted along the demesne wall, a banner headline over the old news of REMEMBER 1690 and NO SURRENDER, a great wingspan of lettering I hurried under with the messages.

In a khaki shirt and brass-buckled belt, a demobbed neighbour leaned against our jamb. My father jingled silver deep in both pockets and laughed when the big clicking rosary beads were produced.

'Did they make a papish of you over there?'

'Oh, damn the fear! I stole them for you, Paddy, off the pope's dresser when his back was turned.'

'You could harness a donkey with them.'

Their laughter sailed above my head, a hoarse clamour, two big nervous birds dipping and lifting, making trial runs over a territory.

Cloistered

tone
Floor

Light was calloused in the leaded panes of the college chapel
and shafted into the terrazzo rink of the sanctuary. The duty
priest tested his diction against pillar and plaster, we tested
our elbows on the hard bevel of the benches or split the gold-
barred thickness of our missals.

I could make a book of hours of those six years, a Flemish
calendar of rite and pastime set on a walled hill. Look: there
is a hillside cemetery behind us and across the river the plough
going in a field and, in between, the gated town. Here, an
obedient clerk kissing a bishop's ring, here a frieze of seasonal
games, and here the assiduous illuminator himself, bowed to
his desk in a corner.

In the study hall my hand was cold as a scribe's in winter.
The supervisor rustled past, sibilant, vapouring into his bre-
viary, his welted.brogues unexpectedly secular under the sou-
tane. Now I bisected the line AB, now found my foothold in
a main verb in Livy. From my dormer after lights-out I revised
the constellations and in the morning broke the ice in an
enamelled water-jug with exhilarated self-regard.

The Stations of the West

On my first night in the Gaeltacht the old woman spoke to me in English: 'You will be all right.' I sat on a twilit bedside listening through the wall to fluent Irish, homesick for a speech I was to extirpate.

I had come west to inhale the absolute weather. The visionaries breathed on my face a smell of soup-kitchens, they mixed the dust of croppies' graves with the fasting spittle of our creed and anointed my lips. *Ephete*, they urged. I blushed but only managed a few words.

Neither did any gift of tongues descend in my days in that upper room when all around me seemed to prophesy. But still I would recall the stations of the west, white sand, hard rock, light ascending like its definition over Rannafast and Errigal, Annaghry and Kincasslagh: names portable as altar stones, unleavened elements.

Incertus

I went disguised in it, pronouncing it with a soft church-Latin *c*, tagging it under my efforts like a damp fuse. Uncertain. A shy soul fretting and all that. Expert obeisance.

Oh yes, I crept before I walked. The old pseudonym lies there like a mouldering tegument.

FROM

North

———————

(1 9 7 5)

Mossbawn

For Mary Heaney

1. Sunlight

There was a sunlit absence.
The helmeted pump in the yard
heated its iron,
water honeyed

in the slung bucket
and the sun stood
like a griddle cooling
against the wall

of each long afternoon.
So, her hands scuffled
over the bakeboard,
the reddening stove

sent its plaque of heat
against her where she stood
in a floury apron
by the window.

Now she dusts the board
with a goose's wing,
now sits, broad-lapped,
with whitened nails

and measling shins:
here is a space

again, the scone rising
to the tick of two clocks.

And here is love
like a tinsmith's scoop
sunk past its gleam
in the meal-bin.

2. *The Seed Cutters*

They seem hundreds of years away. Brueghel,
You'll know them if I can get them true.
They kneel under the hedge in a half-circle
Behind a windbreak wind is breaking through.
They are the seed cutters. The tuck and frill
Of leaf-sprout is on the seed potatoes
Buried under that straw. With time to kill,
They are taking their time. Each sharp knife goes
Lazily halving each root that falls apart
In the palm of the hand: a milky gleam,
And, at the centre, a dark watermark.
Oh, calendar customs! Under the broom
Yellowing over them, compose the frieze
With all of us there, our anonymities.

Funeral Rites

Focus? each one

family

J

I

I shouldered a kind of manhood
stepping in to lift the coffins
of dead relations.
They had been laid out

in tainted rooms,
their eyelids glistening,
their dough-white hands
shackled in rosary beads.

Their puffed knuckles
had unwrinkled, the nails
were darkened, the wrists
obediently sloped.

The dulse-brown shroud,
the quilted-satin cribs:
I knelt courteously
admiring it all

as wax melted down
and veined the candles,
the flames hovering
to the women hovering

behind me.
And always, in a corner,
the coffin lid,
its nail-heads dressed

65

with little gleaming crosses.
Dear soapstone masks,
kissing their igloo brows
had to suffice

before the nails were sunk
and the black glacier
of each funeral
pushed away.

II

Now as news comes in
of each neighbourly murder
we pine for ceremony,
customary rhythms:

the temperate footsteps
of a cortège, winding past
each blinded home.
I would restore

the great chambers of Boyne,
prepare a sepulchre
under the cupmarked stones.
Out of side-streets and by-roads

purring family cars
nose into line,
the whole country tunes
to the muffled drumming

of ten thousand engines.
Somnambulant women,
left behind, move
through emptied kitchens

imagining our slow triumph
towards the mounds.
Quiet as a serpent
in its grassy boulevard,

the procession drags its tail
out of the Gap of the North
as its head already enters
the megalithic doorway.

Norse - Viking Murders

Strongford → Norway
Coolingford

III

When they have put the stone
back in its mouth
we will drive north again
past Strang and Carling fjords,

the cud of memory
allayed for once, arbitration
of the feud placated,
imagining those under the hill

disposed like Gunnar
who lay beautiful
inside his burial mound,
though dead by violence

King of the killings
Volsung Saga

67

and unavenged.
Men said that he was chanting
verses about honour
and that four lights burned

in corners of the chamber:
which opened then, as he turned
with a joyful face
to look at the moon.

North

I returned to a long strand,
the hammered curve of a bay,
and found only the secular
powers of the Atlantic thundering.

I faced the unmagical
invitations of Iceland,
the pathetic colonies
of Greenland, and suddenly

those fabulous raiders,
those lying in Orkney and Dublin
measured against
their long swords rusting,

those in the solid
belly of stone ships,
those hacked and glinting
in the gravel of thawed streams

were ocean-deafened voices
warning me, lifted again
in violence and epiphany.
The longship's swimming tongue

was buoyant with hindsight—
it said Thor's hammer swung
to geography and trade,
thick-witted couplings and revenges,

the hatreds and behindbacks
of the althing, lies and women,
exhaustions nominated peace,
memory incubating the spilled blood.

It said, 'Lie down
in the word-hoard, burrow
the coil and gleam
of your furrowed brain.

Compose in darkness.
Expect aurora borealis
in the long foray
but no cascade of light.

Keep your eye clear
as the bleb of the icicle,
trust the feel of what nubbed treasure
your hands have known.'

Viking Dublin: Trial Pieces

(handwritten: Tale)

I

It could be a jaw-bone
or a rib or a portion cut
from something sturdier:
anyhow, a small outline

was incised, a cage
or trellis to conjure in.
Like a child's tongue
following the toils

of his calligraphy,
like an eel swallowed
in a basket of eels,
the line amazes itself

eluding the hand
that fed it,
a bill in flight,
a swimming nostril.

II

These are trial pieces,
the craft's mystery
improvised on bone:
foliage, bestiaries,

interlacings elaborate
as the netted routes

of ancestry and trade.
That have to be

magnified on display
so that the nostril
is a migrant prow
sniffing the Liffey,

swanning it up to the ford,
dissembling itself
in antler combs, bone pins,
coins, weights, scale-pans.

III

Like a long sword
sheathed in its moisting
burial clays,
the keel stuck fast

in the slip of the bank,
its clinker-built hull
spined and plosive
as *Dublin*.

And now we reach in
for shards of the vertebrae,
the ribs of hurdle,
the mother-wet caches—

and for this trial piece
incised by a child,
a longship, a buoyant
migrant line.

IV

That enters my longhand,
turns cursive, unscarfing
a zoomorphic wake,   *obival forms*
a worm of thought

I follow into the mud.
I am Hamlet the Dane,
skull-handler, parablist,
smeller of rot

in the state, infused
with its poisons,
pinioned by ghosts
and affections,

murders and pieties,
coming to consciousness
by jumping in graves,
dithering, blathering.

V

Come fly with me,
come sniff the wind
with the expertise
of the Vikings—

neighbourly, scoretaking
killers, haggers
and hagglers, gombeen-men,
hoarders of grudges and gain.

73

With a butcher's aplomb
they spread out your lungs
and made you warm wings
for your shoulders.

Old fathers, be with us.
Old cunning assessors
of feuds and of sites
for ambush or town.

VI

'Did you ever hear tell,'
said Jimmy Farrell,
'of the skulls they have
in the city of Dublin?

White skulls and black skulls
and yellow skulls, and some
with full teeth, and some
haven't only but one,'

and compounded history
in the pan of 'an old Dane,
maybe, was drowned
in the Flood.'

My words lick around
cobbled quays, go hunting
lightly as pampooties   *soulals*
over the skull-capped ground.

Bone Dreams

White bone found
on the grazing:
the rough, porous
language of touch

and its yellowing, ribbed
impression in the grass—
a small ship-burial.
As dead as stone,

flint-find, nugget
of chalk,
I touch it again,
I wind it in

the sling of mind
to pitch it at England
and follow its drop
to strange fields.

Bone-house:
a skeleton
in the tongue's
old dungeons.

I push back
through dictions,

Elizabethan canopies,
Norman devices,

the erotic mayflowers
of Provence
and the ivied Latins
of churchmen

to the scop's
twang, the iron
flash of consonants
cleaving the line.

III

In the coffered
riches of grammar
and declensions
I found *bān-hūs*,

its fire, benches,
wattle and rafters,
where the soul
fluttered a while

in the roofspace.
There was a small crock
for the brain,
and a cauldron

of generation
swung at the centre:
love-den, blood-holt,
dream-bower.

IV

Come back past
philology and kennings,
re-enter memory
where the bone's lair

is a love-nest
in the grass.
I hold my lady's head
like a crystal

and ossify myself
by gazing: I am screes
on her escarpments,
a chalk giant

carved upon her downs.
Soon my hands, on the sunken
fosse of her spine,
move towards the passes.

V

And we end up
cradling each other
between the lips
of an earthwork.

As I estimate
for pleasure
her knuckles' paving,
the turning stiles

of the elbows,
the vallum of her brow
and the long wicket
of collar-bone,

I have begun to pace
the Hadrian's Wall
of her shoulder, dreaming
of Maiden Castle.

VI

One morning in Devon
I found a dead mole
with the dew still beading it.
I had thought the mole

a big-boned coulter
but there it was
small and cold
as the thick of a chisel.

I was told 'Blow,
blow back the fur on his head.
Those little points
were the eyes.

And feel the shoulders.'
I touched small distant Pennines,
a pelt of grass and grain
running south.

Bog Queen   *speaking*

I lay waiting
between turf-face and demesne wall,
between heathery levels
and glass-toothed stone.

My body was braille
for the creeping influences:
dawn suns groped over my head
and cooled at my feet,

through my fabrics and skins
the seeps of winter
digested me,
the illiterate roots

pondered and died
in the cavings
of stomach and socket.
I lay waiting

on the gravel bottom,
my brain darkening,
a jar of spawn
fermenting underground

dreams of Baltic amber.
Bruised berries under my nails,
the vital hoard reducing
in the crock of the pelvis.

My diadem grew carious,
gemstones dropped
in the peat floe
like the bearings of history.

My sash was a black glacier
wrinkling, dyed weaves
and Phoenician stitchwork
retted on my breasts'

soft moraines.
I knew winter cold
like the nuzzle of fjords
at my thighs—

the soaked fledge, the heavy
swaddle of hides.
My skull hibernated
in the wet nest of my hair.

Which they robbed.
I was barbered
and stripped
by a turfcutter's spade

who veiled me again
and packed coomb softly
between the stone jambs
at my head and my feet.

Till a peer's wife bribed him.
The plait of my hair,

a slimy birth-cord
of bog, had been cut

and I rose from the dark,
hacked bone, skull-ware,
frayed stitches, tufts,
small gleams on the bank.

The Grauballe Man

cf Tollund
Andrews 85 f.

As if he had been poured
in tar, he lies
on a pillow of turf
and seems to weep

the black river of himself.
The grain of his wrists
is like bog oak,
the ball of his heel

like a basalt egg.
His instep has shrunk
cold as a swan's foot
or a wet swamp root.

His hips are the ridge
and purse of a mussel,
his spine an eel arrested
under a glisten of mud.

The head lifts,
the chin is a visor
raised above the vent
of his slashed throat

that has tanned and toughened.
The cured wound
opens inwards to a dark
elderberry place.

Who will say 'corpse'
to his vivid cast?
Who will say 'body'
to his opaque repose?

And his rusted hair,
a mat unlikely
as a foetus's.
I first saw his twisted face

in a photograph,
a head and shoulder
out of the peat,
bruised like a forceps baby,

but now he lies
perfected in my memory,
down to the red horn
of his nails,

hung in the scales
with beauty and atrocity:
with the Dying Gaul
too strictly compassed

on his shield,
with the actual weight
of each hooded victim,
slashed and dumped.

cf bog —
∂ preservatives

✓

Punishment

I can feel the tug
of the halter at the nape
of her neck, the wind
on her naked front.

It blows her nipples
to amber beads,
it shakes the frail rigging
of her ribs.

I can see her drowned
body in the bog,
the weighing stone,
the floating rods and boughs.

Under which at first
she was a barked sapling
that is dug up
oak-bone, brain-firkin:

her shaved head
like a stubble of black corn,
her blindfold a soiled bandage,
her noose a ring

to store
the memories of love.
Little adulteress,
before they punished you

you were flaxen-haired,
undernourished, and your
tar-black face was beautiful.
My poor scapegoat,

I almost love you
but would have cast, I know,
the stones of silence.
I am the artful voyeur

of your brain's exposed
and darkened combs,
your muscles' webbing
and all your numbered bones:

I who have stood dumb
when your betraying sisters,
cauled in tar,
wept by the railings,

who would connive
in civilized outrage
yet understand the exact
and tribal, intimate revenge.

Strange Fruit

Here is the girl's head like an exhumed gourd.
Oval-faced, prune-skinned, prune-stones for teeth.
They unswaddled the wet fern of her hair
And made an exhibition of its coil,
Let the air at her leathery beauty.
Pash of tallow, perishable treasure:
Her broken nose is dark as a turf clod,
Her eyeholes blank as pools in the old workings.
Diodorus Siculus confessed
His gradual ease among the likes of this:
Murdered, forgotten, nameless, terrible
Beheaded girl, outstaring axe
And beatification, outstaring
What had begun to feel like reverence.

Act of Union

(handwritten annotations: "sex: politics too pol?" / "puns" / "(Irish Background)")

I

To-night, a first movement, a pulse,
As if the rain in bogland gathered head
To slip and flood: a bog-burst,
A gash breaking open the ferny bed.
Your back is a firm line of eastern coast
And arms and legs are thrown
Beyond your gradual hills. I caress
The heaving province where our past has grown.
I am the tall kingdom over your shoulder
That you would neither cajole nor ignore.
Conquest is a lie. I grow older
Conceding your half-independent shore
Within whose borders now my legacy
Culminates inexorably.

II

And I am still imperially
Male, leaving you with the pain,
The rending process in the colony,
The battering ram, the boom burst from within.
The act sprouted an obstinate fifth column
Whose stance is growing unilateral.
His heart beneath your heart is a wardrum
Mustering force. His parasitical
And ignorant little fists already
Beat at your borders and I know they're cocked
At me across the water. No treaty

I foresee will salve completely your tracked
And stretchmarked body, the big pain
That leaves you raw, like opened ground, again.

Hercules and Antaeus

*colourer /
coloured*

Sky-born and royal,
snake-choker, dung-heaver,
his mind big with golden apples,
his future hung with trophies,

Hercules has the measure
of resistance and black powers
feeding off the territory.
Antaeus, the mould-hugger,

is weaned at last:
a fall was a renewal
but now he is raised up—
the challenger's intelligence

is a spur of light,
a blue prong graiping him
out of his element
into a dream of loss

and origins—the cradling dark,
the river-veins, the secret gullies
of his strength,
the hatching grounds

of cave and souterrain,
he has bequeathed it all
to elegists. Balor will die
and Byrthnoth and Sitting Bull.

*Natives defeat-
by conquerers*

89

Hercules lifts his arms
in a remorseless V,
his triumph unassailed
by the powers he has shaken,

and lifts and banks Antaeus
high as a profiled ridge,
a sleeping giant,
pap for the dispossessed.

From *Whatever You Say Say Nothing*

I

I'm writing this just after an encounter
With an English journalist in search of 'views
On the Irish thing'. I'm back in winter
Quarters where bad news is no longer news,

Where media-men and stringers sniff and point,
Where zoom lenses, recorders and coiled leads
Litter the hotels. The times are out of joint
But I incline as much to rosary beads

As to the jottings and analyses
Of politicians and newspapermen
Who've scribbled down the long campaign from gas
And protest to gelignite and Sten,

Who proved upon their pulses 'escalate',
'Backlash' and 'crack-down', 'the provisional wing',
'Polarization' and 'long-standing hate'.
Yet I live here, I live here too, I sing,

Expertly civil-tongued with civil neighbours
On the high wires of first wireless reports,
Sucking the fake taste, the stony flavours
Of those sanctioned, old, elaborate retorts:

'Oh, it's disgraceful, surely, I agree,'
'Where's it going to end?' 'It's getting worse.'
'They're murderers.' 'Internment, understandably . . .'
The 'voice of sanity' is getting hoarse.

'Religion's never mentioned here,' of course.
'You know them by their eyes,' and hold your tongue.
'One side's as bad as the other,' never worse.
Christ, it's near time that some small leak was sprung

In the great dykes the Dutchman made
To dam the dangerous tide that followed Seamus.
Yet for all this art and sedentary trade
I am incapable. The famous

Northern reticence, the tight gag of place
And times: yes, yes. Of the 'wee six' I sing
Where to be saved you only must save face
And whatever you say, you say nothing.

Smoke-signals are loud-mouthed compared with us:
Manoeuvrings to find out name and school,
Subtle discrimination by addresses
With hardly an exception to the rule

That Norman, Ken and Sidney signalled Prod
And Seamus (call me Sean) was sure-fire Pape.
O land of password, handgrip, wink and nod,
Of open minds as open as a trap,

Where tongues lie coiled, as under flames lie wicks,
Where half of us, as in a wooden horse,
Were cabin'd and confined like wily Greeks,
Besieged within the siege, whispering morse.

IV

This morning from a dewy motorway
I saw the new camp for the internees:
A bomb had left a crater of fresh clay
In the roadside, and over in the trees

Machine-gun posts defined a real stockade.
There was that white mist you get on a low ground
And it was déjà-vu, some film made
Of Stalag 17, a bad dream with no sound.

Is there a life before death? That's chalked up
In Ballymurphy. Competence with pain,
Coherent miseries, a bite and sup,
We hug our little destiny again.

From *Singing School*

*dialect os
pol*, *erbure,*
rel. *identity*

Fair seedtime had my soul, and I grew up
Fostered alike by beauty and by fear;
Much favoured in my birthplace, and no less
In that beloved Vale to which, erelong,
I was transplanted . . .

—WILLIAM WORDSWORTH, *The Prelude*

He [the stable-boy] had a book of Orange
rhymes, and the days when we read them
together in the hay-loft gave me the
pleasure of rhyme for the first time. Later on
I can remember being told, when there was
a rumour of a Fenian rising, that rifles were
being handed out to the Orangemen; and
presently, when I began to dream of my
future life, I thought I would like to die
fighting the Fenians.

—W. B. YEATS, *Autobiographies*

94

what's new?
Does it work?

1. The Ministry of Fear

For Seamus Deane

Well, as Kavanagh said, we have lived
In important places. The lonely scarp
Of St Columb's College, where I billeted
For six years, overlooked your Bogside.
I gazed into new worlds: the inflamed throat
Of Brandywell, its floodlit dogtrack,
The throttle of the hare. In the first week
I was so homesick I couldn't even eat
The biscuits left to sweeten my exile.
I threw them over the fence one night
In September 1951
When the lights of houses in the Lecky Road
Were amber in the fog. It was an act
Of stealth.
            Then Belfast, and then Berkeley.
Here's two on's are sophisticated,
Dabbling in verses till they have become
A life: from bulky envelopes arriving
In vacation time to slim volumes
Despatched 'with the author's compliments'.
Those poems in longhand, ripped from the wire spine
Of your exercise book, bewildered me—
Vowels and ideas bandied free
As the seed-pods blowing off our sycamores.
I tried to write about the sycamores
And innovated a South Derry rhyme
With *hushed* and *lulled* full chimes for *pushed* and *pulled*.

Those hobnailed boots from beyond the mountain
Were walking, by God, all over the fine
Lawns of elocution.
                           Have our accents
Changed? 'Catholics, in general, don't speak
As well as students from the Protestant schools.'
Remember that stuff? Inferiority
Complexes, stuff that dreams were made on.
'What's your name, Heaney?'
                                          'Heaney, Father.'
                                                        'Fair

Enough.'
                  On my first day, the leather strap
Went epileptic in the Big Study,
Its echoes plashing over our bowed heads,
But I still wrote home that a boarder's life
Was not so bad, shying as usual.

On long vacations, then, I came to life
In the kissing seat of an Austin 16
Parked at a gable, the engine running,
My fingers tight as ivy on her shoulders,
A light left burning for her in the kitchen.
And heading back for home, the summer's
Freedom dwindling night by night, the air
All moonlight and a scent of hay, policemen
Swung their crimson flashlamps, crowding round
The car like black cattle, snuffing and pointing
The muzzle of a Sten gun in my eye:
'What's your name, driver?'
                                       'Seamus . . .'
                                                 Seamus?
They once read my letters at a roadblock
And shone their torches on your hieroglyphics,
'Svelte dictions' in a very florid hand.

Ulster was British, but with no rights on
The English lyric: all around us, though
We hadn't named it, the ministry of fear.

2. A Constable Calls

His bicycle stood at the window-sill,
The rubber cowl of a mud-splasher
Skirting the front mudguard,
Its fat black handlegrips

Heating in sunlight, the 'spud'
Of the dynamo gleaming and cocked back,
The pedal treads hanging relieved
Of the boot of the law.

His cap was upside down
On the floor, next his chair.
The line of its pressure ran like a bevel
In his slightly sweating hair.

He had unstrapped
The heavy ledger, and my father
Was making tillage returns
In acres, roods and perches.

Arithmetic and fear.
I sat staring at the polished holster
With its buttoned flap, the braid cord
Looped into the revolver butt.

'Any other root crops?
Mangolds? Marrowstems? Anything like that?'
'No.' But was there not a line
Of turnips where the seed ran out

In the potato field? I assumed
Small guilts and sat
Imagining the black hole in the barracks.
He stood up, shifted the baton-case

Further round on his belt,
Closed the domesday book,
Fitted his cap back with two hands,
And looked at me as he said goodbye.

A shadow bobbed in the window.
He was snapping the carrier spring
Over the ledger. His boot pushed off
And the bicycle ticked, ticked, ticked.

Again, how " political " ?

4. Summer 1969

While the Constabulary covered the mob
Firing into the Falls, I was suffering
Only the bullying sun of Madrid.
Each afternoon, in the casserole heat
Of the flat, as I sweated my way through
The life of Joyce, stinks from the fishmarket
Rose like the reek off a flax-dam.
At night on the balcony, gules of wine,
A sense of children in their dark corners,
Old women in black shawls near open windows,
The air a canyon rivering in Spanish.
We talked our way home over starlit plains
Where patent leather of the Guardia Civil
Gleamed like fish-bellies in flax-poisoned waters.

'Go back,' one said, 'try to touch the people.'
Another conjured Lorca from his hill.
We sat through death counts and bullfight reports
On the television, celebrities
Arrived from where the real thing still happened.

I retreated to the cool of the Prado.
Goya's 'Shootings of the Third of May'
Covered a wall—the thrown-up arms
And spasm of the rebel, the helmeted
And knapsacked military, the efficient
Rake of the fusillade. In the next room
His nightmares, grafted to the palace wall—
Dark cyclones, hosting, breaking; Saturn

Jewelled in the blood of his own children,
Gigantic Chaos turning his brute hips
Over the world. Also, that holmgang
Where two berserks club each other to death
For honour's sake, greaved in a bog, and sinking.

He painted with his fists and elbows, flourished
The stained cape of his heart as history charged.

5. Fosterage

For Michael McLaverty

'Description is revelation!' Royal
Avenue, Belfast, 1962,
A Saturday afternoon, glad to meet
Me, newly cubbed in language, he gripped
My elbow. 'Listen. Go your own way.
Do your own work. Remember
Katherine Mansfield—*I will tell
How the laundry basket squeaked* . . . that note of exile.'
But to hell with overstating it:
'Don't have the veins bulging in your Biro.'
And then, 'Poor Hopkins!' I have the *Journals*
He gave me, underlined, his buckled self
Obeisant to their pain. He discerned
The lineaments of patience everywhere
And fostered me and sent me out, with words
Imposing on my tongue like obols. *Silver coins*

6. Exposure

It is December in Wicklow:
Alders dripping, birches
Inheriting the last light,
The ash tree cold to look at.

A comet that was lost
Should be visible at sunset,
Those million tons of light
Like a glimmer of haws and rose-hips,

[handwritten margin note: hawthorne fruit]

And I sometimes see a falling star.
If I could come on meteorite!
Instead I walk through damp leaves,
Husks, the spent flukes of autumn,

[handwritten margin note: flat fish or barb of an anchor]

Imagining a hero
On some muddy compound,
His gift like a slingstone
Whirled for the desperate.

How did I end up like this?
I often think of my friends'
Beautiful prismatic counselling
And the anvil brains of some who hate me

As I sit weighing and weighing
My responsible *tristia*.
For what? For the ear? For the people?
For what is said behind-backs?

103

Rain comes down through the alders,
Its low conducive voices
Mutter about let-downs and erosions
And yet each drop recalls

The diamond absolutes.
I am neither internee nor informer;
An inner émigré, grown long-haired
And thoughtful; a wood-kerne

Escaped from the massacre
Taking protective colouring
From bole and bark, feeling
Every wind that blows;

Who, blowing up these sparks
For their meagre heat, have missed
The once-in-a-lifetime portent,
The comet's pulsing rose.

F R O M

Field Work

———————————

(1 9 7 9)

Pleasurepoint
s krl. at Colby   (?)

Oysters

Our shells clacked on the plates.
My tongue was a filling estuary,
My palate hung with starlight:
As I tasted the salty Pleiades
Orion dipped his foot into the water.

Alive and violated
They lay on their beds of ice:
Bivalves: the split bulb
And philandering sigh of ocean.
Millions of them ripped and shucked and scattered.

We had driven to that coast
Through flowers and limestone
And there we were, toasting friendship,
Laying down a perfect memory
In the cool of thatch and crockery.

Over the Alps, packed deep in hay and snow,
The Romans hauled their oysters south to Rome:
I saw damp panniers disgorge
The frond-lipped, brine-stung
Glut of privilege

And was angry that my trust could not repose
In the clear light, like poetry or freedom
Leaning in from sea. I ate the day
Deliberately, that its tang
Might quicken me all into verb, pure verb.

3 diff responses re Troubles — IA, 137

British Ambassador Christopher Ewart Biggs, 1976

Triptych

I

After a Killing

There they were, as if our memory hatched them,
As if the unquiet founders walked again:
Two young men with rifles on the hill,
Profane and bracing as their instruments.

Image 1

Who's sorry for our trouble?
Who dreamt that we might dwell among ourselves
In rain and scoured light and wind-dried stones?
Basalt, blood, water, headstones, leeches.

In that neuter original loneliness
From Brandon to Dunseverick
I think of small-eyed survivor flowers,
The pined-for, unmolested orchid.

Image 2

I see a stone house by a pier.
Elbow room. Broad window light.
The heart lifts. You walk twenty yards
To the boats and buy mackerel.

And to-day a girl walks in home to us
Carrying a basket full of new potatoes,
Three tight green cabbages, and carrots
With the tops and mould still fresh on them.

Image 3

Relationship away Images?

II

Sibyl

My tongue moved, a swung relaxing hinge.
I said to her, 'What will become of us?'
And as forgotten water in a well might shake
At an explosion under morning

Or a crack run up a gable,
She began to speak.
'I think our very form is bound to change.
Dogs in a siege. Saurian relapses. Pismires.

Unless forgiveness finds its nerve and voice,
Unless the helmeted and bleeding tree
Can green and open buds like infants' fists
And the fouled magma incubate

Bright nymphs . . . My people think money
And talk weather. Oil-rigs lull their future
On single acquisitive stems. Silence
Has shoaled into the trawlers' echo-sounders.

The ground we kept our ear to for so long
Is flayed or calloused, and its entrails
Tented by an impious augury.
Our island is full of comfortless noises.'

III

At the Water's Edge

On Devenish I heard a snipe
And the keeper's recital of elegies
Under the tower. Carved monastic heads
Were crumbling like bread on water.

On Boa the god-eyed, sex-mouthed stone
Socketed between graves, two-faced, trepanned,
Answered my silence with silence.
A stoup for rain water. Anathema.

From a cold hearthstone on Horse Island
I watched the sky beyond the open chimney
And listened to the thick rotations
Of an army helicopter patrolling.

A hammer and a cracked jug full of cobwebs
Lay on the window-sill. Everything in me
Wanted to bow down, to offer up,
To go barefoot, foetal and penitential,

And pray at the water's edge.
How we crept before we walked! I remembered
The helicopter shadowing our march at Newry,
The scared, irrevocable steps.

110

The Toome Road

One morning early I met armoured cars
In convoy, warbling along on powerful tyres,
All camouflaged with broken alder branches,
And headphoned soldiers standing up in turrets.
How long were they approaching down my roads
As if they owned them? The whole country was sleeping.
I had rights-of-way, fields, cattle in my keeping,
Tractors hitched to buckrakes in open sheds,
Silos, chill gates, wet slates, the greens and reds
Of outhouse roofs. Whom should I run to tell
Among all of those with their back doors on the latch
For the bringer of bad news, that small-hours visitant
Who, by being expected, might be kept distant?
Sowers of seed, erectors of headstones . . .
O charioteers, above your dormant guns,
It stands here still, stands vibrant as you pass,
The invisible, untoppled omphalos.

A Drink of Water

She came every morning to draw water
Like an old bat staggering up the field:
The pump's whooping cough, the bucket's clatter
And slow diminuendo as it filled,
Announced her. I recall
Her grey apron, the pocked white enamel
Of the brimming bucket, and the treble
Creak of her voice like the pump's handle.
Nights when a full moon lifted past her gable
It fell back through her window and would lie
Into the water set out on the table.
Where I have dipped to drink again, to be
Faithful to the admonishment on her cup,
Remember the Giver fading off the lip.

The Strand at Lough Beg

In Memory of Colum McCartney

> *All round this little island, on the strand*
> *Far down below there, where the breakers strive,*
> *Grow the tall rushes from the oozy sand.*
> —DANTE, *Purgatorio, I, 100–3*

Leaving the white glow of filling stations
And a few lonely streetlamps among fields
You climbed the hills towards Newtownhamilton
Past the Fews Forest, out beneath the stars—
Along that road, a high, bare pilgrim's track
Where Sweeney fled before the bloodied heads,
Goat-beards and dogs' eyes in a demon pack
Blazing out of the ground, snapping and squealing.
What blazed ahead of you? A faked roadblock?
The red lamp swung, the sudden brakes and stalling
Engine, voices, heads hooded and the cold-nosed gun?
Or in your driving mirror, tailing headlights
That pulled out suddenly and flagged you down
Where you weren't known and far from what you knew:
The lowland clays and waters of Lough Beg,
Church Island's spire, its soft treeline of yew.

There you once heard guns fired behind the house
Long before rising time, when duck shooters
Haunted the marigolds and bulrushes,
But still were scared to find spent cartridges,
Acrid, brassy, genital, ejected,

113

On your way across the strand to fetch the cows.
For you and yours and yours and mine fought shy,
Spoke an old language of conspirators
And could not crack the whip or seize the day:
Big-voiced scullions, herders, feelers round
Haycocks and hindquarters, talkers in byres,
Slow arbitrators of the burial ground.

Across that strand of yours the cattle graze
Up to their bellies in an early mist
And now they turn their unbewildered gaze
To where we work our way through squeaking sedge
Drowning in dew. Like a dull blade with its edge
Honed bright, Lough Beg half shines under the haze.
I turn because the sweeping of your feet
Has stopped behind me, to find you on your knees
With blood and roadside muck in your hair and eyes,
Then kneel in front of you in brimming grass
And gather up cold handfuls of the dew
To wash you, cousin. I dab you clean with moss
Fine as the drizzle out of a low cloud.
I lift you under the arms and lay you flat.
With rushes that shoot green again, I plait
Green scapulars to wear over your shroud.

Casualty

cf born "Dooker"
" Station Island

Lovers O'Neill - old
acquaintance — EH 125

I

He would drink by himself
And raise a weathered thumb
Towards the high shelf,
Calling another rum
And blackcurrant, without
Having to raise his voice,
Or order a quick stout
By a lifting of the eyes
And a discreet dumb-show
Of pulling off the top;
At closing time would go
In waders and peaked cap
Into the showery dark,
A dole-kept breadwinner
But a natural for work.
I loved his whole manner,
Sure-footed but too sly,
His deadpan sidling tact,
His fisherman's quick eye
And turned observant back.

Incomprehensible
To him, my other life.
Sometimes, on his high stool,
Too busy with his knife
At a tobacco plug
And not meeting my eye,
In the pause after a slug
He mentioned poetry.

We would be on our own
And, always politic
And shy of condescension,
I would manage by some trick
To switch the talk to eels
Or lore of the horse and cart
Or the Provisionals.

But my tentative art
His turned back watches too:
He was blown to bits
Out drinking in a curfew
Others obeyed, three nights
After they shot dead
The thirteen men in Derry.
PARAS THIRTEEN, the walls said,
BOGSIDE NIL. That Wednesday
Everybody held
His breath and trembled.

II

It was a day of cold
Raw silence, wind-blown
Surplice and soutane:
Rained-on, flower-laden
Coffin after coffin
Seemed to float from the door
Of the packed cathedral
Like blossoms on slow water.
The common funeral
Unrolled its swaddling band,
Lapping, tightening

Till we were braced and bound
Like brothers in a ring.

But he would not be held
At home by his own crowd
Whatever threats were phoned,
Whatever black flags waved.
I see him as he turned
In that bombed offending place,
Remorse fused with terror
In his still knowable face,
His cornered outfaced stare
Blinding in the flash.

He had gone miles away
For he drank like a fish
Nightly, naturally
Swimming towards the lure
Of warm lit-up places,
The blurred mesh and murmur
Drifting among glasses
In the gregarious smoke.
How culpable was he
That last night when he broke
Our tribe's complicity?
'Now, you're supposed to be
An educated man,'
I hear him say. 'Puzzle me
The right answer to that one.'

III

I missed his funeral,
Those quiet walkers

And sideways talkers
Shoaling out of his lane
To the respectable
Purring of the hearse . . .
They move in equal pace
With the habitual
Slow consolation
Of a dawdling engine,
The line lifted, hand
Over fist, cold sunshine
On the water, the land
Banked under fog: that morning
When he took me in his boat,
The screw purling, turning
Indolent fathoms white,
I tasted freedom with him.
To get out early, haul
Steadily off the bottom,
Dispraise the catch, and smile
As you find a rhythm
Working you, slow mile by mile,
Into your proper haunt
Somewhere, well out, beyond . . .

Dawn-sniffing revenant,
Plodder through midnight rain,
Question me again.

The Badgers

When the badger glimmered away
into another garden
you stood, half-lit with whiskey,
sensing you had disturbed
some soft returning.

The murdered dead,
you thought.
But could it not have been
some violent shattered boy
nosing out what got mislaid
between the cradle and the explosion,
evenings when windows stood open
and the compost smoked down the backs?

Visitations are taken for signs.
At a second house I listened
for duntings under the laurels
and heard intimations whispered
about being vaguely honoured.

And to read even by carcasses
the badgers have come back.
One that grew notorious
lay untouched in the roadside.
Last night one had me braking
but more in fear than in honour.

Cool from the sett and redolent
of his runs under the night,
the bogey of fern country
broke cover in me
for what he is:
pig family
and not at all what he's painted.

How perilous is it to choose
not to love the life we're shown?
His sturdy dirty body
and interloping grovel.
The intelligence in his bone.
The unquestionable houseboy's shoulders
that could have been my own.

The Singer's House

When they said *Carrickfergus* I could hear
the frosty echo of saltminers' picks.
I imagined it, chambered and glinting,
a township built of light.

What do we say any more
to conjure the salt of our earth?
So much comes and is gone
that should be crystal and kept,

and amicable weathers
that bring up the grain of things,
their tang of season and store,
are all the packing we'll get.

So I say to myself *Gweebarra*
and its music hits off the place
like water hitting off granite.
I see the glittering sound

framed in your window,
knives and forks set on oilcloth,
and the seals' heads, suddenly outlined,
scanning everything.

People here used to believe
that drowned souls lived in the seals.
At spring tides they might change shape.
They loved music and swam in for a singer

who might stand at the end of summer
in the mouth of a whitewashed turf-shed,
his shoulder to the jamb, his song
a rowboat far out in evening.

When I came here first you were always singing,
a hint of the clip of the pick
in your winnowing climb and attack.
Raise it again, man. We still believe what we hear.

The Guttural Muse

Late summer, and at midnight
I smelt the heat of the day:
At my window over the hotel car park
I breathed the muddied night airs off the lake
And watched a young crowd leave the discotheque.

Their voices rose up thick and comforting
As oily bubbles the feeding tench sent up
That evening at dusk—the slimy tench
Once called the 'doctor fish' because his slime
Was said to heal the wounds of fish that touched it.

A girl in a white dress
Was being courted out among the cars:
As her voice swarmed and puddled into laughs
I felt like some old pike all badged with sores
Wanting to swim in touch with soft-mouthed life.

Glanmore Sonnets

For Ann Saddlemyer,
our heartiest welcomer

I

Vowels ploughed into other: opened ground.
The mildest February for twenty years
Is mist bands over furrows, a deep no sound
Vulnerable to distant gargling tractors.
Our road is steaming, the turned-up acres breathe.
Now the good life could be to cross a field
And art a paradigm of earth new from the lathe
Of ploughs. My lea is deeply tilled.
Old ploughsocks gorge the subsoil of each sense
And I am quickened with a redolence
Of farmland as a dark unblown rose.
Wait then . . . Breasting the mist, in sowers' aprons,
My ghosts come striding into their spring stations.
The dream grain whirls like freakish Easter snows.

Sensings, mountings from the hiding places,
Words entering almost the sense of touch
Ferreting themselves out of their dark hutch—
'These things are not secrets but mysteries,'
Oisin Kelly told me years ago
In Belfast, hankering after stone
That connived with the chisel, as if the grain
Remembered what the mallet tapped to know.
Then I landed in the hedge-school of Glanmore
And from the backs of ditches hoped to raise
A voice caught back off slug-horn and slow chanter
That might continue, hold, dispel, appease:
Vowels ploughed into other, opened ground,
Each verse returning like the plough turned round.

III

This evening the cuckoo and the corncrake
(So much, too much) consorted at twilight.
It was all crepuscular and iambic.
Out on the field a baby rabbit
Took his bearings, and I knew the deer
(I've seen them too from the window of the house,
Like connoisseurs, inquisitive of air)
Were careful under larch and May-green spruce.
I had said earlier, 'I won't relapse
From this strange loneliness I've brought us to.
Dorothy and William—' She interrupts:
'You're not going to compare us two . . . ?'
Outside a rustling and twig-combing breeze
Refreshes and relents. Is cadences.

IV

I used to lie with an ear to the line
For that way, they said, there should come a sound
Escaping ahead, an iron tune
Of flange and piston pitched along the ground,
But I never heard that. Always, instead,
Struck couplings and shuntings two miles away
Lifted over the woods. The head
Of a horse swirled back from a gate, a grey
Turnover of haunch and mane, and I'd look
Up to the cutting where she'd soon appear.
Two fields back, in the house, small ripples shook
Silently across our drinking water
(As they are shaking now across my heart)
And vanished into where they seemed to start.

V

Soft corrugations in the boortree's trunk,
Its green young shoots, its rods like freckled solder:
It was our bower as children, a greenish, dank
And snapping memory as I get older.
And elderberry I have learned to call it.
I love its blooms like saucers brimmed with meal,
Its berries a swart caviar of shot,
A buoyant spawn, a light bruised out of purple.
Elderberry? It is shires dreaming wine.
Boortree is bower tree, where I played 'touching tongues'
And felt another's texture quick on mine.
So, etymologist of roots and graftings,
I fall back to my tree-house and would crouch
Where small buds shoot and flourish in the hush.

VI

He lived there in the unsayable lights.
He saw the fuchsia in a drizzling noon,
The elderflower at dusk like a risen moon
And green fields greying on the windswept heights.
'I will break through,' he said, 'what I glazed over
With perfect mist and peaceful absences'—
Sudden and sure as the man who dared the ice
And raced his bike across the Moyola River.
A man we never saw. But in that winter
Of nineteen forty-seven, when the snow
Kept the country bright as a studio,
In a cold where things might crystallize or founder,
His story quickened us, a wild white goose
Heard after dark above the drifted house.

VII

Dogger, Rockall, Malin, Irish Sea:
Green, swift upsurges, North Atlantic flux
Conjured by that strong gale-warning voice,
Collapse into a sibilant penumbra.
Midnight and closedown. Sirens of the tundra,
Of eel-road, seal-road, keel-road, whale-road, raise
Their wind-compounded keen behind the baize
And drive the trawlers to the lee of Wicklow.
L'Etoile, Le Guillemot, La Belle Hélène
Nursed their bright names this morning in the bay
That toiled like mortar. It was marvellous
And actual, I said out loud, 'A haven,'
The word deepening, clearing, like the sky
Elsewhere on Minches, Cromarty, The Faroes.

VIII

Thunderlight on the split logs: big raindrops
At body heat and lush with omen
Spattering dark on the hatchet iron.
This morning when a magpie with jerky steps
Inspected a horse asleep beside the wood
I thought of dew on armour and carrion.
What would I meet, blood-boltered, on the road?
How deep into the woodpile sat the toad?
What welters through this dark hush on the crops?
Do you remember that *pension* in Les Landes
Where the old one rocked and rocked and rocked
A mongol in her lap, to little songs?
Come to me quick, I am upstairs shaking.
My all of you birchwood in lightning.

Outside the kitchen window a black rat
Sways on the briar like infected fruit:
'It looked me through, it stared me out, I'm not
Imagining things. Go you out to it.'
Did we come to the wilderness for this?
We have our burnished bay tree at the gate,
Classical, hung with the reek of silage
From the next farm, tart-leafed as inwit.
Blood on a pitchfork, blood on chaff and hay,
Rats speared in the sweat and dust of threshing—
What is my apology for poetry?
The empty briar is swishing
When I come down, and beyond, inside, your face
Haunts like a new moon glimpsed through tangled glass.

X

I dreamt we slept in a moss in Donegal
On turf banks under blankets, with our faces
Exposed all night in a wetting drizzle,
Pallid as the dripping sapling birches.
Lorenzo and Jessica in a cold climate.
Diarmuid and Grainne waiting to be found.
Darkly asperged and censed, we were laid out
Like breathing effigies on a raised ground.
And in that dream I dreamt—how like you this?—
Our first night years ago in that hotel
When you came with your deliberate kiss
To raise us towards the lovely and painful
Covenants of flesh; our separateness;
The respite in our dewy dreaming faces.

sprinkled w holy water.

An Afterwards

another domestic self-destruction.

She would plunge all poets in the ninth circle
And fix them, tooth in skull, tonguing for brain;
For backbiting in life she'd make their hell
A rabid egotistical daisy-chain.

Unyielding, spurred, ambitious, unblunted,
Lockjawed, mantrapped, each a fastened badger
Jockeying for position, hasped and mounted
Like Ugolino on Archbishop Roger.

And when she'd make her circuit of the ice,
Aided and abetted by Virgil's wife,
I would cry out, 'My sweet, who wears the bays
In our green land above, whose is the life

Most dedicated and exemplary?'
And she: 'I have closed my widowed ears
To the sulphurous news of poets and poetry.
Why could you not have, oftener, in our years

Unclenched, and come down laughing from your room
And walked the twilight with me and your children—
Like that one evening of elder bloom
And hay, when the wild roses were fading?'

And (as some maker gaffs me in the neck)
'You weren't the worst. You aspired to a kind,
Indifferent, faults-on-both-sides tact.
You left us first, and then those books, behind.'

The Otter

When you plunged
The light of Tuscany wavered
And swung through the pool
From top to bottom.

I loved your wet head and smashing crawl,
Your fine swimmer's back and shoulders
Surfacing and surfacing again
This year and every year since.

I sat dry-throated on the warm stones.
You were beyond me.
The mellowed clarities, the grape-deep air
Thinned and disappointed.

Thank God for the slow loadening,
When I hold you now
We are close and deep
As the atmosphere on water.

My two hands are plumbed water.
You are my palpable, lithe
Otter of memory
In the pool of the moment,

Turning to swim on your back,
Each silent, thigh-shaking kick
Retilting the light,
Heaving the cool at your neck.

And suddenly you're out,
Back again, intent as ever,
Heavy and frisky in your freshened pelt,
Printing the stones.

The Skunk

Up, black, striped and damasked like the chasuble
At a funeral Mass, the skunk's tail
Paraded the skunk. Night after night
I expected her like a visitor.

The refrigerator whinnied into silence.
My desk light softened beyond the verandah.
Small oranges loomed in the orange tree.
I began to be tense as a voyeur.

After eleven years I was composing
Love-letters again, broaching the word 'wife'
Like a stored cask, as if its slender vowel
Had mutated into the night earth and air

Of California. The beautiful, useless
Tang of eucalyptus spelt your absence.
The aftermath of a mouthful of wine
Was like inhaling you off a cold pillow.

And there she was, the intent and glamorous,
Ordinary, mysterious skunk,
Mythologized, demythologized,
Snuffing the boards five feet beyond me.

It all came back to me last night, stirred
By the sootfall of your things at bedtime,
Your head-down, tail-up hunt in a bottom drawer
For the black plunge-line nightdress.

A Dream of Jealousy

Walking with you and another lady
In wooded parkland, the whispering grass
Ran its fingers through our guessing silence
And the trees opened into a shady
Unexpected clearing where we sat down.
I think the candour of the light dismayed us.
We talked about desire and being jealous,
Our conversation a loose single gown
Or a white picnic tablecloth spread out
Like a book of manners in the wilderness.
'Show me,' I said to our companion, 'what
I have much coveted, your breast's mauve star.'
And she consented. Oh, neither these verses
Nor my prudence, love, can heal your wounded stare.

From *Field Work*

I

Where the sally tree went pale in every breeze,
where the perfect eye of the nesting blackbird watched,
where one fern was always green

I was standing watching you
take the pad from the gatehouse at the crossing
and reach to lift a white wash off the whins.

I could see the vaccination mark
stretched on your upper arm, and smell the coal smell
of the train that comes between us, a slow goods,

waggon after waggon full of big-eyed cattle.

III

Not the mud slick,
not the black weedy water
full of alder cones and pock-marked leaves.

Not the cow parsley in winter
with its old whitened shins and wrists,
its sibilance, its shaking.

Not even the tart green shade of summer
thick with butterflies
and fungus plump as a leather saddle.

No. But in a still corner,
braced to its pebble-dashed wall,
heavy, earth-drawn, all mouth and eye,

the sunflower, dreaming umber.

IV

Catpiss smell,
the pink bloom open:
I press a leaf
of the flowering currant
on the back of your hand
for the tight slow burn
of its sticky juice
to prime your skin,
and your veins to be crossed
criss-cross with leaf-veins.
I lick my thumb
and dip it in mould,
I anoint the anointed
leaf-shape. Mould
blooms and pigments
the back of your hand
like a birthmark—
my umber one,
you are stained, stained
to perfection.

c. 1977

Song

berry of wt. osy

A rowan like a lipsticked girl.
Between the by-road and the main road
Alder trees at a wet and dripping distance
Stand off among the rushes.

There are the mud-flowers of dialect
And the immortelles of perfect pitch
And that moment when the bird sings very close
To the music of what happens.

The Harvest Bow

As you plaited the harvest bow
You implicated the mellowed silence in you
In wheat that does not rust
But brightens as it tightens twist by twist
Into a knowable corona,
A throwaway love-knot of straw.

Hands that aged round ash plants and cane sticks
And lapped the spurs on a lifetime of gamecocks
Harked to their gift and worked with fine intent
Until your fingers moved somnambulant:
I tell and finger it like braille,
Gleaning the unsaid off the palpable,

And if I spy into its golden loops
I see us walk between the railway slopes
Into an evening of long grass and midges,
Blue smoke straight up, old beds and ploughs in hedges,
An auction notice on an outhouse wall—
You with a harvest bow in your lapel,

Me with the fishing rod, already homesick
For the big lift of these evenings, as your stick
Whacking the tips off weeds and bushes
Beats out of time, and beats, but flushes
Nothing: that original townland
Still tongue-tied in the straw tied by your hand.

The end of art is peace
Could be the motto of this frail device
That I have pinned up on our deal dresser—
Like a drawn snare
Slipped lately by the spirit of the corn
Yet burnished by its passage, and still warm.

In Memoriam Francis Ledwidge

Killed in France 31 July 1917

The bronze soldier hitches a bronze cape
That crumples stiffly in imagined wind
No matter how the real winds buff and sweep
His sudden hunkering run, forever craned

Over Flanders. Helmet and haversack,
The gun's firm slope from butt to bayonet,
The loyal, fallen names on the embossed plaque—
It all meant little to the worried pet

I was in nineteen forty-six or seven,
Gripping my Aunt Mary by the hand
Along the Portstewart prom, then round the crescent
To thread the Castle Walk out to the strand.

The pilot from Coleraine sailed to the coal-boat.
Courting couples rose out of the scooped dunes.
A farmer stripped to his studs and shiny waistcoat
Rolled the trousers down on his timid shins.

Francis Ledwidge, you courted at the seaside
Beyond Drogheda one Sunday afternoon.
Literary, sweet-talking, countrified,
You pedalled out the leafy road from Slane

Where you belonged, among the dolorous
And lovely: the May altar of wild flowers,
Easter water sprinkled in outhouses,
Mass-rocks and hill-top raths and raftered byres.

I think of you in your Tommy's uniform,
A haunted Catholic face, pallid and brave,
Ghosting the trenches like a bloom of hawthorn
Or silence cored from a Boyne passage-grave.

It's summer, nineteen-fifteen. I see the girl
My aunt was then, herding on the long acre.
Behind a low bush in the Dardanelles
You suck stones to make your dry mouth water.

It's nineteen-seventeen. She still herds cows
But a big strafe puts the candles out in Ypres:
'My soul is by the Boyne, cutting new meadows . . .
My country wears her confirmation dress.'

'To be called a British soldier while my country
Has no place among nations . . .' You were rent
By shrapnel six weeks later. 'I am sorry
That party politics should divide our tents.'

In you, our dead enigma, all the strains
Criss-cross in useless equilibrium
And as the wind tunes through this vigilant bronze
I hear again the sure confusing drum

You followed from Boyne water to the Balkans
But miss the twilit note your flute should sound.
You were not keyed or pitched like these true-blue ones
Though all of you consort now underground.

cf WBY, P.6 Sequence "Reprisals" esp

145

FROM

Sweeney Astray

(1 9 8 3)

For notes, as marked, Andrews 146 –

Sweeney Praises the Trees

It was the end of the harvest season and Sweeney heard a hunting-call from a company in the skirts of the wood.

—This will be the outcry of the Ui Faolain coming to kill me, he said. I slew their king at Moira and this host is out to avenge him.

He heard the stag bellowing and he made a poem in which he praised aloud all the trees of Ireland, and rehearsed some of his own hardships and sorrows, saying:

Suddenly this bleating
and belling in the glen!
The little timorous stag
like a scared musician

startles my heartstrings
with high homesick refrains—
deer on my lost mountains,
flocks out on the plain.

The bushy leafy oak tree
is highest in the wood,
the forking shoots of hazel
hide sweet hazel-nuts.

The alder is my darling,
all thornless in the gap,
some milk of human kindness
coursing in its sap.

The blackthorn is a jaggy creel
stippled with dark sloes;
green watercress in thatch on wells
where the drinking blackbird goes.

Sweetest of the leafy stalks,
the vetches strew the pathway;
the oyster-grass is my delight,
and the wild strawberry.

Low-set clumps of apple trees
drum down fruit when shaken;
scarlet berries clot like blood
on mountain rowan.

Briars curl in sideways,
arch a stickle back,
draw blood and curl up innocent
to sneak the next attack.

The yew tree in each churchyard
wraps night in its dark hood.
Ivy is a shadowy
genius of the wood.

Holly rears its windbreak,
a door in winter's face;
life-blood on a spear-shaft
darkens the grain of ash.

Birch tree, smooth and blessed,
delicious to the breeze,

high twigs plait and crown it
the queen of trees.

The aspen pales
and whispers, hesitates:
a thousand frightened scuts
race in its leaves.

But what disturbs me most
in the leafy wood
is the to and fro and to and fro
of an oak rod.

Sweeney Astray

I would live happy
in an ivy bush
high in some twisted tree
and never come out.

The skylarks rising
to their high space
send me pitching and tripping
over stumps on the moor

and my hurry flushes
the turtle-dove.
I overtake it,
my plumage rushing,

am startled
by the startled woodcock
or a blackbird's sudden
volubility.

Think of my alarms,
my coming to earth
where the fox still
gnaws at the bones,

my wild career
as the wolf from the wood
goes tearing ahead
and I lift towards the mountain,

the bark of foxes
echoing below me,
the wolves behind me
howling and rending—

their vapoury tongues,
their low-slung speed
shaken off like nightmare
at the foot of the slope.

If I show my heels
I am hobbled by guilt.
I am a sheep
without a fold

who sleeps his sound sleep
in the old tree at Kilnoo,
dreaming back the good days
with Congal in Antrim.

A starry frost will come
dropping on pools
and I'll be astray here
on unsheltered heights:

herons calling
in cold Glenelly,
flocks of birds quickly
coming and going.

I prefer the elusive
rhapsody of blackbirds

to the garrulous blather
of men and women.

I prefer the squeal of badgers
in their sett
to the tally-ho
of the morning hunt.

I prefer the re-
echoing belling of a stag
among the peaks
to that arrogant horn.

Those unharnessed runners
from glen to glen!
Nobody tames
that royal blood,

each one aloof
on its rightful summit,
antlered, watchful.
Imagine them,

the stag of high Slieve Felim,
the stag of the steep Fews,
the stag of Duhallow, the stag of Orrery,
the fierce stag of Killarney.

The stag of Islandmagee, Larne's stag,
the stag of Moylinny,
the stag of Cooley, the stag of Cunghill,
the stag of the two-peaked Burren.

The mother of this herd
is old and grey,
the stags that follow her
are branchy, many-tined.

I would be cloaked in the grey
sanctuary of her head,
I would roost among
her mazy antlers

and would be lofted into
this thicket of horns
on the stag that lows at me
over the glen.

I am Sweeney, the whinger,
the scuttler in the valley.
But call me, instead,
Peak-pate, Stag-head.

Sweeney's Lament on Ailsa Craig

Without bed or board
I face dark days
in frozen lairs
and wind-driven snow.

Ice scoured by winds.
Watery shadows from weak sun.
Shelter from the one tree
on a plateau.

Haunting deer-paths,
enduring rain,
first-footing the grey
frosted grass.

I climb towards the pass
and the stag's belling
rings off the wood,
surf-noise rises

where I go, heartbroken
and worn out,
sharp-haunched Sweeney,
raving and moaning.

The sough of the winter night,
my feet packing the hailstones
as I pad the dappled
banks of Mourne

or lie, unslept, in a wet bed
on the hills by Lough Erne,
tensed for first light
and an early start.

Skimming the waves
at Dunseverick,
listening to billows
at Dun Rodairce,

hurtling from that great wave
to the wave running
in tidal Barrow,
one night in hard Dun Cernan,

the next among the wild flowers
of Benn Boirne;
and then a stone pillow
on the screes of Croagh Patrick.

But to have ended up
lamenting here
on Ailsa Craig.
A hard station!

Ailsa Craig,
the seagulls' home,
God knows it is
hard lodgings.

Ailsa Craig,
bell-shaped rock,

reaching sky-high,
snout in the sea—

it hard-beaked,
me seasoned and scraggy:
we mated like a couple
of hard-shanked cranes.

Sweeney in Connacht

One day Sweeney went to Drum Iarann in Connacht, where
he stole some watercress and drank from a green-flecked well.
A cleric came out of the church, full of indignation and re-
sentment, calling Sweeney a well-fed, contented madman,
and reproaching him where he cowered in the yew tree:

Cleric:
Aren't you the contented one?
You eat my watercress,
then you perch in the yew tree
beside my little house.

Sweeney:
Contented's not the word!
I am so terrified,
so panicky, so haunted
I dare not bat an eyelid.

The flight of a small wren
scares me as much, bell-man,
as a great expedition
out to hunt me down.

Were you in my place, monk,
and I in yours, think:
would you enjoy being mad?
Would you be contented?

Once when Sweeney was rambling and raking through Connacht he ended up in Alternan in Tireragh. A community of holy people had made their home there, and it was a lovely valley, with a turbulent river shooting down the cliff; trees fruited and blossomed on the cliff-face; there were sheltering ivies and heavy-topped orchards, there were wild deer and hares and fat swine; and sleek seals, that used to sleep on the cliff, having come in from the ocean beyond. Sweeney coveted the place mightily and sang its praises aloud in this poem:

Sainted cliff at Alternan,
nut grove, hazel-wood!
Cold quick sweeps of water
fall down the cliff-side.

Ivies green and thicken there,
its oak-mast is precious.
Fruited branches nod and bend
from heavy-headed apple trees.

Badgers make their setts there
and swift hares have their form;
and seals' heads swim the ocean,
cobbling the running foam.

And by the waterfall, Colman's son,
haggard, spent, frost-bitten Sweeney,
Ronan of Drumgesh's victim,
is sleeping at the foot of a tree.

Sweeney's Last Poem

There was a time when I preferred
the turtle-dove's soft jubilation
as it flitted round a pool
to the murmur of conversation.

There was a time when I preferred
the blackbird singing on the hill
and the stag loud against the storm
to the clinking tongue of this bell.

There was a time when I preferred
the mountain grouse crying at dawn
to the voice and closeness
of a beautiful woman.

There was a time when I preferred
wolf-packs yelping and howling
to the sheepish voice of a cleric
bleating out plainsong.

You are welcome to pledge healths
and carouse in your drinking dens;
I will dip and steal water
from a well with my open palm.

You are welcome to that cloistered hush
of your students' conversation;
I will study the pure chant
of hounds baying in Glen Bolcain.

You are welcome to your salt meat
and fresh meat in feasting-houses;
I will live content elsewhere
on tufts of green watercress.

The herd's sharp spear wounded me
and passed clean through my body.
Ah Christ, who disposed all things, why
was I not killed at Moira?

Of all the innocent lairs I made
the length and breadth of Ireland
I remember an open bed
above the lough in Mourne.

Of all the innocent lairs I made
the length and breadth of Ireland
I remember bedding down
above the wood in Glen Bolcain.

To you, Christ, I give thanks
for your Body in communion.
Whatever evil I have done
in this world, I repent.

Then Sweeney's death-swoon came over him and Moling,
attended by his clerics, rose up and each of them placed a
stone on Sweeney's grave.

F R O M

Station Island

(1 9 8 4)

The Underground

There we were in the vaulted tunnel running,
You in your going-away coat speeding ahead
And me, me then like a fleet god gaining
Upon you before you turned to a reed

Or some new white flower japped with crimson
As the coat flapped wild and button after button
Sprang off and fell in a trail
Between the Underground and the Albert Hall.

Honeymooning, mooning around, late for the Proms,
Our echoes die in that corridor and now
I come as Hansel came on the moonlit stones
Retracing the path back, lifting the buttons

To end up in a draughty lamplit station
After the trains have gone, the wet track
Bared and tensed as I am, all attention
For your step following and damned if I look back.

Sloe Gin

The clear weather of juniper
darkened into winter.
She fed gin to sloes
and sealed the glass container.

When I unscrewed it
I smelled the disturbed
tart stillness of a bush
rising through the pantry.

When I poured it
it had a cutting edge
and flamed
like Betelgeuse.

I drink to you
in smoke-mirled, blue-black,
polished sloes, bitter
and dependable.

Chekhov on Sakhalin

For Derek Mahon

So, he would pay his 'debt to medicine'.
But first he drank cognac by the ocean
With his back to all he travelled north to face.
His head was swimming free as the troikas

Of Tyumin, he looked down from the rail
Of his thirty years and saw a mile
Into himself as if he were clear water:
Lake Baikal from the deckrail of the steamer.

So far away, Moscow was like lost youth.
And who was he, to savour in his mouth
Fine spirits that the puzzled literati
Packed off with him to a penal colony—

Him, born, you may say, under the counter?
At least that meant he knew its worth. No cantor
In full throat by the iconostasis
Got holier joy than he got from that glass

That shone and warmed like diamonds warming
On some pert young cleavage in a salon,
Inviolable and affronting.
He felt the glass go cold in the midnight sun.

When he staggered up and smashed it on the stones
It rang as clearly as the convicts' chains
That haunted him. All through the months to come
It rang on like the burden of his freedom

167

To try for the right tone—not tract, not thesis—
And walk away from floggings. He who thought to squeeze
His slave's blood out and waken the free man
Shadowed a convict guide through Sakhalin.

Sandstone Keepsake

It is a kind of chalky russet
solidified gourd, sedimentary
and so reliably dense and bricky
I often clasp it and throw it from hand to hand.

It was ruddier, with an underwater
hint of contusion, when I lifted it,
wading a shingle beach on Inishowen.
Across the estuary light after light

came on silently round the perimeter
of the camp. A stone from Phlegethon,
bloodied on the bed of hell's hot river?
Evening frost and the salt water

made my hand smoke, as if I'd plucked the heart
that damned Guy de Montfort to the boiling flood—
but not really, though I remembered
his victim's heart in its casket, long venerated.

Anyhow, there I was with the wet red stone
in my hand, staring across at the watch-towers
from my free state of image and allusion,
swooped on, then dropped by trained binoculars:

a silhouette not worth bothering about,
out for the evening in scarf and waders
and not about to set times wrong or right,
stooping along, one of the venerators.

From *Shelf Life*

Granite Chip

Houndstooth stone. Aberdeen of the mind.

Saying *An union in the cup I'll throw*
I have hurt my hand, pressing it hard around
this bit hammered off Joyce's Martello
Tower, this flecked insoluble brilliant

I keep but feel little in common with—
a kind of stone-age circumcising knife,
a Calvin edge in my complaisant pith.
Granite is jaggy, salty, punitive

and exacting. *Come to me*, it says
*all you who labour and are burdened, I
will not refresh you.* And it adds, *Seize
the day.* And, *You can take me or leave me.*

Old Smoothing Iron

Often I watched her lift it
from where its compact wedge
rode the back of the stove
like a tug at anchor.

To test its heat she'd stare
and spit in its iron face
or hold it up next her cheek
to divine the stored danger.

Soft thumps on the ironing board.
Her dimpled angled elbow
and intent stoop
as she aimed the smoothing iron

like a plane into linen,
like the resentment of women.
To work, her dumb lunge says,
is to move a certain mass

through a certain distance,
is to pull your weight and feel
exact and equal to it.
Feel dragged upon. And buoyant.

Stone from Delphi

To be carried back to the shrine some dawn
when the sea spreads its far sun-crops to the south
and I make a morning offering again:
that I may escape the miasma of spilled blood,
govern the tongue, fear hybris, fear the god
until he speaks in my untrammelled mouth.

Making Strange

I stood between them,
the one with his travelled intelligence
and tawny containment,
his speech like the twang of a bowstring,

and another, unshorn and bewildered
in the tubs of his wellingtons,
smiling at me for help,
faced with this stranger I'd brought him.

Then a cunning middle voice
came out of the field across the road
saying, 'Be adept and be dialect,
tell of this wind coming past the zinc hut,

call me sweetbriar after the rain
or snowberries cooled in the fog.
But love the cut of this travelled one
and call me also the cornfield of Boaz.

Go beyond what's reliable
in all that keeps pleading and pleading,
these eyes and puddles and stones,
and recollect how bold you were

when I visited you first
with departures you cannot go back on.'
A chaffinch flicked from an ash and next thing
I found myself driving the stranger

through my own country, adept
at dialect, reciting my pride
in all that I knew, that began to make strange
at that same recitation.

A Hazel Stick for Catherine Ann

The living mother-of-pearl of a salmon
just out of the water

is gone just like that, but your stick
is kept salmon-silver.

Seasoned and bendy,
it convinces the hand

that what you have you hold
to play with and pose with

and lay about with.
But then too it points back to cattle

and spatter and beating
the bars of a gate—

the very stick we might cut
from your family tree.

The living cobalt of an afternoon
dragonfly drew my eye to it first

and the evening I trimmed it for you
you saw your first glow-worm—

all of us stood round in silence, even you
gigantic enough to darken the sky

for a glow-worm.
And when I poked open the grass

a tiny brightening den lit the eye
in the blunt cut end of your stick.

A Kite for Michael and Christopher

All through that Sunday afternoon
a kite flew above Sunday,
a tightened drumhead, an armful of blown chaff.

I'd seen it grey and slippy in the making,
I'd tapped it when it dried out white and stiff,
I'd tied the bows of newspaper
along its six-foot tail.

But now it was far up like a small black lark
and now it dragged as if the bellied string
were a wet rope hauled upon
to lift a shoal.

My friend says that the human soul
is about the weight of a snipe,
yet the soul at anchor there,
the string that sags and ascends,
weigh like a furrow assumed into the heavens.

Before the kite plunges down into the wood
and this line goes useless
take in your two hands, boys, and feel
the strumming, rooted, long-tailed pull of grief.
You were born fit for it.
Stand in here in front of me
and take the strain.

The Railway Children

When we climbed the slopes of the cutting
We were eye-level with the white cups
Of the telegraph poles and the sizzling wires.

Like lovely freehand they curved for miles
East and miles west beyond us, sagging
Under their burden of swallows.

We were small and thought we knew nothing
Worth knowing. We thought words travelled the wires
In the shiny pouches of raindrops,

Each one seeded full with the light
Of the sky, the gleam of the lines, and ourselves
So infinitesimally scaled

We could stream through the eye of a needle.

bird ?
worker ?

The King of the Ditchbacks

For John Montague

I

As if a trespasser
unbolted a forgotten gate
and ripped the growth
tangling its lower bars—

just beyond the hedge
he has opened a dark morse
along the bank,
a crooked wounding

of silent, cobwebbed
grass. If I stop
he stops
like the moon.

He lives in his feet
and ears, weather-eyed,
all pad and listening,
a denless mover.

Under the bridge
his reflection shifts
sideways to the current,
mothy, alluring.

I am haunted
by his stealthy rustling,

the unexpected spoor,
the pollen settling.

II

I was sure I knew him. The time I'd spent obsessively in that
upstairs room bringing myself close to him: each entranced
hiatus as I chainsmoked and stared out the dormer into the
grassy hillside I was laying myself open. He was depending
on me as I hung out on the limb of a translated phrase like
a youngster dared out onto an alder branch over the whirlpool.
Small dreamself in the branches. Dream fears I inclined to-
wards, interrogating:

—Are you the one I ran upstairs to find drowned under
running water in the bath?
—The one the mowing machine severed like a hare in the
stiff frieze of harvest?
—Whose little bloody clothes we buried in the garden?
—The one who lay awake in darkness a wall's breadth from
the troubled hoofs?

After I had dared these invocations, I went back towards the
gate to follow him. And my stealth was second nature to me,
as if I were coming into my own. I remembered I had been
vested for this calling.

III

When I was taken aside that day
I had the sense of election:

they dressed my head in a fishnet
and plaited leafy twigs through meshes

so my vision was a bird's
at the heart of a thicket

and I spoke as I moved
like a voice from a shaking bush.

King of the ditchbacks,
I went with them obediently

to the edge of a pigeon wood—
deciduous canopy, screened wain of evening

we lay beneath in silence.
No birds came, but I waited

among briars and stones, or whispered
or broke the watery gossamers

if I moved a muscle.
'Come back to us,' they said, 'in harvest,

when we hide in the stooked corn,
when the gundogs can hardly retrieve

what's brought down.' And I saw myself
rising to move in that dissimulation,

top-knotted, masked in sheaves, noting
the fall of birds: a rich young man

leaving everything he had
for a migrant solitude.

Sit + Scene — Tension

Station Island

I

A hurry of bell-notes
flew over morning hush
and water-blistered cornfields,
an escaped ringing
that stopped as quickly

Lough Derg ?
Atmosphere ?
changes –

as it started. *Sunday,*
the silence breathed
and could not settle back
for a man had appeared
at the side of the field

with a bow-saw, held
stiffly up like a lyre.
He moved and stopped to gaze
up into hazel bushes,
angled his saw in,

pulled back to gaze again
and move on to the next.
'I know you, Simon Sweeney,
for an old Sabbath-breaker
who has been dead for years.'

Figure from childhood.
Woodcutter, rural craftsman
cf. Sweeney story

'Damn all you know,' he said,
his eye still on the hedge
and not turning his head.
'I was your mystery man
and am again this morning.

Through gaps in the bushes,
your First Communion face
would watch me cutting timber.
When cut or broken limbs
of trees went yellow, when

woodsmoke sharpened air
or ditches rustled
you sensed my trail there
as if it had been sprayed.
It left you half afraid.

When they bade you listen
in the bedroom dark
to wind and rain in the trees
and think of tinkers camped
under a heeled-up cart

you shut your eyes and saw
a wet axle and spokes
in moonlight, and me
streaming from the shower,
headed for your door.'

Sunlight broke in the hazels,
the quick bell-notes began
a second time. I turned
at another sound:
a crowd of shawled women

were wading the young corn,
their skirts brushing softly.
Their motion saddened morning.

It whispered to the silence,
'Pray for us, pray for us,'

it conjured through the air
until the field was full
of half-remembered faces,
a loosed congregation
that straggled past and on.

As I drew behind them
I was a fasted pilgrim,
light-headed, leaving home
to face into my station.
'Stay clear of all processions!'

Sweeney shouted at me
but the murmur of the crowd
and their feet slushing through
the tender, bladed growth
had opened a drugged path

I was set upon.
I trailed those early-risers
fallen into step
before the smokes were up.
The quick bell rang again.

Tension:
- ghosts o what they say.
- Pilgrims r what they do
- SH's consciousness

Wm Carleton: was last
convert: RC to Prot.
satirist

of Joyce of

XII

Presence
srl reaction
exchange, p 186

Trails & Stories of īc
Irish Peasantry

wrnt on īc pilgrimage.

II

Satire
ver
always
Lough Derg.

I was parked on a high road, listening
to peewits and wind blowing round the car
when something came to life in the driving mirror,

someone walking fast in an overcoat
and boots, bareheaded, big, determined
in his sure haste along the crown of the road

so that I felt myself the challenged one.
The car door slammed. I was suddenly out
face to face with an aggravated man

raving on about nights spent listening for
gun butts to come cracking on the door,
yeomen on the rampage, and his neighbour

among them, hammering home the shape of things.
'Round about here you overtook the women,'
I said, as the thing came clear. 'Your *Lough Derg Pilgrim*

but

haunts me every time I cross this mountain—
as if I am being followed, or following.
I'm on my road there now to do the station.'

'O holy Jesus Christ, does nothing change?'
His head jerked sharply side to side and up
like a diver's surfacing,

184

then with a look that said, *Who is this cub*
anyhow, he took cognizance again
of where he was: the road, the mountain top,

and the air, softened by a shower of rain,
worked on his anger visibly until:
'It is a road you travel on your own.

I who learned to read in the reek of flax
and smelled hanged bodies rotting on their gibbets
and saw their looped slime gleaming from the sacks—

hard-mouthed Ribbonmen and Orange bigots
made me into the old fork-tongued turncoat
who mucked the byre of their politics.

If times were hard, I could be hard too.
I made the traitor in me sink the knife.
And maybe there's a lesson there for you,

whoever you are, wherever you come out of,
for though there's something natural in your smile
there's something in it strikes me as defensive.'

'The angry role was never my vocation,'
I said. 'I come from County Derry,
where the last marching bands of Ribbonmen

on Patrick's Day still played their "Hymn to Mary".
Obedient strains like theirs tuned me first
and not that harp of unforgiving iron

the Fenians strung. A lot of what you wrote
I heard and did: this Lough Derg station,
flax-pullings, dances, fair-days, crossroads chat

and the shaky local voice of education.
All that. And always, Orange drums.
And neighbours on the roads at night with guns.'

'I know, I know, I know, I know,' he said,
'but you have to try to make sense of what comes.
Remember everything and keep your head.'

'The alders in the hedge,' I said, 'mushrooms,
dark-clumped grass where cows or horses dunged,
the cluck when pith-lined chestnut shells split open

in your hand, the melt of shells corrupting,
old jam pots in a drain clogged up with mud—'
But now Carleton was interrupting:

'All this is like a trout kept in a spring
or maggots sown in wounds—
another life that cleans our element.

We are earthworms of the earth, and all that
has gone through us is what will be our trace.'
He turned on his heel when he was saying this

and headed up the road at the same hard pace.

III

I knelt. Hiatus. Habit's afterlife . . .
I was back among bead clicks and the murmurs
from inside confessionals, side altars
where candles died insinuating slight

intimate smells of wax at body heat.
There was an active, wind-stilled hush, as if
in a shell the listened-for ocean stopped
and a tide rested and sustained the roof.

A seaside trinket floated then and idled
in vision, like phosphorescent weed,
a toy grotto with seedling mussel shells
and cockles glued in patterns over it,

pearls condensed from a child invalid's breath
into a shimmering ark, my house of gold
that housed the snowdrop weather of her death
long ago. I would stow away in the hold

of our big oak sideboard and forage for it
laid past in its tissue paper for good.
It was like touching birds' eggs, robbing the nest
of the word *wreath*, as kept and dry and secret

as her name, which they hardly ever spoke
but was a white bird trapped inside me
beating scared wings when *Health of the Sick*
fluttered its *pray for us* in the litany.

A cold draught blew under the kneeling boards.
I thought of walking round
and round a space utterly empty,
utterly a source, like the idea of sound

or like the absence sensed in swamp-fed air
above a ring of walked-down grass and rushes
where we once found the bad carcass and scrags of hair
of our dog that had disappeared weeks before.

lost invisible ?

Young Friend
Priest who has
lost his vocation.
? (Life) in missionary work.
? challenges his pilgrimage

IV

Blurred swimmings as I faced the sun, my back
to the stone pillar and the iron cross,
ready to say the dream words *I renounce* . . .

Blurred oval prints of newly ordained faces,
'Father' pronounced with a fawning relish,
the sunlit tears of parents being blessed.

I saw a young priest, glossy as a blackbird,
as if he had stepped from his anointing
a moment ago: his purple stole and cord

or cincture tied loosely, his polished shoes
unexpectedly secular beneath
a pleated, lace-hemmed alb of linen cloth.

His name had lain undisturbed for years
like an old bicycle wheel in a ditch
ripped at last from under jungling briars,

wet and perished. My arms were open wide
but I could not say the words. 'The rain forest,' he said,
'you've never seen the like of it. I lasted

only a couple of years. Bare-breasted
women and rat-ribbed men. Everything wasted.
I rotted like a pear. I sweated Masses . . .'

189

His breath came short and shorter. 'In longhouses
I raised the chalice above headdresses.
In hoc signo . . . On that abandoned

mission compound, my vocation
is a steam off drenched creepers.'
I had broken off from the renunciation

while he was speaking, to clear the way
for other pilgrims queueing to get started.
'I'm older now than you when you went away,'

I ventured, feeling a strange reversal.
'I never could see you on the foreign missions.
I could only see you on a bicycle,

a clerical student home for the summer
doomed to the decent thing. Visiting neighbours.
Drinking tea and praising home-made bread.

Something in them would be ratified
when they saw you at the door in your black suit,
arriving like some sort of holy mascot.

You gave too much relief, you raised a siege
the world had laid against their kitchen grottoes
hung with holy pictures and crucifixes.'

'And you,' he faltered, 'what are you doing here
but the same thing? What possessed you?
I at least was young and unaware

that what I thought was chosen was convention.
But all this you were clear of you walked into
over again. And the god has, as they say, withdrawn.

What are you doing, going through these motions?
Unless . . . Unless . . .' Again he was short of breath
and his whole fevered body yellowed and shook.

'Unless you are here taking the last look.'
Then where he stood was empty as the roads
we both grew up beside, where the sick man

had taken his last look one drizzly evening
when the tarmac steamed with the first breath of spring,
a knee-deep mist I waded silently

behind him, on his circuits, visiting.

V

An old man's hands, like soft paws rowing forward,
groped for and warded off the air ahead.
Barney Murphy shuffled on the concrete.
Master Murphy. I heard the weakened voice
bulling in sudden rage all over again
and fell in behind, my eyes fixed on his heels
like a man lifting swathes at a mower's heels.
His sockless feet were like the dried broad bean
that split its stitches in the display jar
high on a window in the old classroom,
white as shy faces in the classroom door.
'Master,' those elders whispered, 'I wonder, master . . .'
rustling envelopes, proffering them, withdrawing,
waiting for him to sign beside their mark,
and 'Master' I repeated to myself
so that he stopped but did not turn or move,
gone quiet in the shoulders, his small head
vigilant in the cold gusts off the lough.
I moved ahead and faced him, shook his hand.

Above the winged collar, his mottled face
went distant in a smile as the voice
readied itself and husked and scraped, 'Good man,
good man yourself,' before it lapsed again
in the limbo and dry urn of the larynx.
The Adam's apple in its weathered sac
worked like the plunger of a pump in drought
but yielded nothing to help the helpless smile.
Morning field smells came past on the wind,

the sex-cut of sweetbriar after rain,
new-mown meadow hay, birds' nests filled with leaves.
'You'd have thought that Anahorish School
was purgatory enough for any man,'
I said. 'You have done your station.'
Then a little trembling happened and his breath
rushed the air softly as scythes in his lost meadows.
'Birch trees have overgrown Leitrim Moss,
dairy herds are grazing where the school was
and the school garden's loose black mould is grass.'
He was gone with that and I was faced wrong way
into more pilgrims absorbed in this exercise.
As I stood among their whispers and bare feet
the mists of all the mornings I set out
for Latin classes with him, face to face,
refreshed me. *Mensa, mensa, mensam*
sang in the air like a busy sharping-stone.

'We'll go some day to my uncle's farm at Toome—'
Another master spoke. *'For what is the great
moving power and spring of verse? Feeling, and
in particular, love.* When I went last year
I drank three cups of water from the well.
It was very cold. It stung me in the ears.
You should have met him—' Coming in as usual
with the rubbed quotation and his cocked bird's eye
dabbing for detail. *When you're on the road
give lifts to people, you'll always learn something.*
There he went, in his belted gaberdine,
and after him, a third fosterer,
slack-shouldered and clear-eyed: 'Sure I might have known
once I had made the pad, you'd be after me
sooner or later. Forty-two years on
and you've got no farther! But after that again,

[handwritten marginal notes:] Patrick Kovonogh Great Hunger . . . our history poem (The Parish) (the Mother)

[handwritten at bottom:] writer of deep r bowel odure . . . W ue r Lough Dog — publ. portcworck 1942.

where else would you go? Iceland, maybe? Maybe the
   Dordogne?'

And then the parting shot. 'In my own day
the odd one came here on the hunt for women.'

VI

Freckle-face, fox-head, pod of the broom,
Catkin-pixie, little fern-swish:
Where did she arrive from?
Like a wish wished
And gone, her I chose at 'secrets'
And whispered to. When we were playing houses.
I was sunstruck at the basilica door—
A stillness far away, a space, a dish,
A blackened tin and knocked-over stool—
Like a tramped neolithic floor
Uncovered among dunes where the bent grass
Whispers on like reeds about Midas's
Secrets, secrets. I shut my ears to the bell.
Head hugged. Eyes shut. Leaf ears. *Don't tell. Don't tell.*

A stream of pilgrims answering the bell
Trailed up the steps as I went down them
Towards the bottle-green, still
Shade of an oak. Shades of the Sabine farm
On the beds of Saint Patrick's Purgatory.
Late summer, country distance, not an air:
Loosen the toga for wine and poetry
Till Phoebus returning routs the morning star.
As a somnolent hymn to Mary rose
I felt an old pang that bags of grain
And the sloped shafts of forks and hoes
Once mocked me with, at my own long virgin
Fasts and thirsts, my nightly shadow feasts,
Haunting the granaries of words like *breasts.*

195

As if I knelt for years at a keyhole
Mad for it, and all that ever opened
Was the breathed-on grille of a confessional
Until that night I saw her honey-skinned
Shoulder-blades and the wheatlands of her back
Through the wide keyhole of her keyhole dress
And a window facing the deep south of luck
Opened and I inhaled the land of kindness.
As little flowers that were all bowed and shut
By the night chills rise on their stems and open
As soon as they have felt the touch of sunlight,
So I revived in my own wilting powers
And my heart flushed, like somebody set free.
Translated, given, under the oak tree.

Storekeeper/ Friend/ Victim
Murdered by IRA Terrorists —also rundown
Terze rime r both down ... rdown
                              > p 199

VII

I had come to the edge of the water,
soothed by just looking, idling over it
as if it were a clear barometer

or a mirror, when his reflection
did not appear but I sensed a presence
entering into my concentration

on not being concentrated as he spoke
my name. And though I was reluctant
I turned to meet his face and the shock

is still in me at what I saw. His brow
was blown open above the eye and blood
had dried on his neck and cheek. 'Easy now,'

he said, 'it's only me. You've seen men as raw
after a football match . . . What time it was
when I was wakened up I still don't know

but I heard this knocking, knocking, and it
scared me, like the phone in the small hours,
so I had the sense not to put on the light

but looked out from behind the curtain.
I saw two customers on the doorstep
and an old Land Rover with the doors open

parked on the street, so I let the curtain drop;
but they must have been waiting for it to move
for they shouted to come down into the shop.

She started to cry then and roll round the bed,
lamenting and lamenting to herself,
not even asking who it was. "Is your head

astray, or what's come over you?" I roared, more
to bring myself to my senses
than out of any real anger at her,

for the knocking shook me, the way they kept it up,
and her whingeing and half-screeching made it worse.
All the time they were shouting, "Shop!

Shop!" so I pulled on my shoes and a sportscoat
and went back to the window and called out,
"What do you want? Could you quieten the racket

or I'll not come down at all." "There's a child not well.
Open up and see what you have got—pills
or a powder or something in a bottle,"

one of them said. He stepped back off the footpath
so I could see his face in the streetlamp
and when the other moved I knew them both.

But bad and all as the knocking was, the quiet
hit me worse. She was quiet herself now,
lying dead still, whispering to watch out.

At the bedroom door I switched on the light.
"It's odd they didn't look for a chemist.
Who are they anyway at this time of the night?"

she asked me, with the eyes standing in her head.
"I know them to see," I said, but something
made me reach and squeeze her hand across the bed

before I went downstairs into the aisle
of the shop. I stood there, going weak
in the legs. I remember the stale smell

of cooked meat or something coming through
as I went to open up. From then on
you know as much about it as I do.'

'Did they say nothing?' 'Nothing. What would they say?'
'Were they in uniform? Not masked in any way?'
'They were barefaced as they would be in the day,

shites thinking they were the be-all and the end-all.'
'Not that it is any consolation,
but they were caught,' I told him, 'and got jail.'

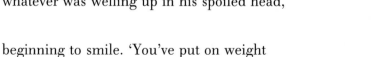

Big-limbed, decent, open-faced, he stood
forgetful of everything now except
whatever was welling up in his spoiled head,

beginning to smile. 'You've put on weight
since you did your courting in that big Austin
you got the loan of on a Sunday night.'

Through life and death he had hardly aged.
There always was an athlete's cleanliness
shining off him, and except for the ravaged

forehead and the blood, he was still that same
rangy midfielder in a blue jersey
and starched pants, the one stylist on the team,

the perfect, clean, unthinkable victim.
'Forgive the way I have lived indifferent—
forgive my timid circumspect involvement,'

I surprised myself by saying. 'Forgive
my eye,' he said, 'all that's above my head.'
And then a stun of pain seemed to go through him

and he trembled like a heatwave and faded.

Figures : a) Friend, Tom, the archaeologist who
died at 37 — (cf. "Strand of Lough Beg "113

b) cousin, Colum McCartney, shot by
Protectors)

2 Tough questions - not forgiving

VIII

Black water. White waves. Furrows snowcapped.
A magpie flew from the basilica
and staggered in the granite airy space
I was staring into, on my knees
at the hard mouth of Saint Brigid's Bed.
I came to and there at the bed's stone hub
was my archaeologist, very like himself,
with his scribe's face smiling its straight-lipped smile,
starting at the sight of me with the same old
pretence of amazement, so that the wing
of wood-kerne's hair fanned down over his brow.
And then as if a shower were blackening
already blackened stubble, the dark weather
of his unspoken pain came over him.
A pilgrim bent and whispering on his rounds
inside the bed passed between us slowly.

ancient
Irish
soldier

'Those dreamy stars that pulsed across the screen
beside you in the ward—your heartbeats, Tom, I mean—
scared me the way they stripped things naked.
My banter failed too early in that visit.
I could not take my eyes off the machine.
I had to head back straightaway to Dublin,
guilty and empty, feeling I had said nothing
and that, as usual, I had somehow broken
covenants, and failed an obligation.
I half-knew we would never meet again . . .
Did our long gaze and last handshake contain
nothing to appease that recognition?'

'Nothing at all. But familiar stone
had me half-numbed to face the thing alone.
I loved my still-faced archaeology.
The small crab-apple physiognomies
on high crosses, carved heads in abbeys . . .
Why else dig in for years in that hard place
in a muck of bigotry under the walls
picking through shards and Williamite cannon balls?
But all that we just turned to banter too.
I felt that I should have seen far more of you
and maybe would have—but dead at thirty-two!
Ah poet, lucky poet, tell me why
what seemed deserved and promised passed me by?'

I could not speak. I saw a hoard of black
basalt axe heads, smooth as a beetle's back,
a cairn of stone force that might detonate,
the eggs of danger. And then I saw a face
he had once given me, a plaster cast
of an abbess, done by the Gowran master,
mild-mouthed and cowled, a character of grace.
'Your gift will be a candle in our house.'
But he had gone when I looked to meet his eyes
and hunkering instead there in his place
was a bleeding, pale-faced boy, plastered in mud.
'The red-hot pokers blazed a lovely red
in Jerpoint the Sunday I was murdered,'
he said quietly. 'Now do you remember?
You were there with poets when you got the word
and stayed there with them, while your own flesh and blood
was carted to Bellaghy from the Fews.
They showed more agitation at the news
than you did.'
                    'But they were getting crisis

first-hand, Colum, they had happened in on
live sectarian assassination.

I was dumb, encountering what was destined.'
And so I pleaded with my second cousin.
'I kept seeing a grey stretch of Lough Beg
and the strand empty at daybreak.
I felt like the bottom of a dried-up lake.'

'You saw that, and you wrote that—not the fact.
You confused evasion and artistic tact.
The Protestant who shot me through the head
I accuse directly, but indirectly, you
who now atone perhaps upon this bed
for the way you whitewashed ugliness and drew
the lovely blinds of the *Purgatorio*
and saccharined my death with morning dew.'

Then I seemed to waken out of sleep
among more pilgrims whom I did not know
drifting to the hostel for the night.

ghosts bring unanswerable questions - of why

R.C. Terrorist – hunger strike – of Bobby Sands
(From work of a daughter?)

IX

'My brain dried like spread turf, my stomach
Shrank to a cinder and tightened and cracked.
Often I was dogs on my own track
Of blood on wet grass that I could have licked.
Under the prison blanket, an ambush
Stillness I felt safe in settled round me.
Streetlights came on in small towns, the bomb flash
Came before the sound, I saw country
I knew from Glenshane down to Toome
And heard a car I could make out years away
With me in the back of it like a white-faced groom,
A hit-man on the brink, emptied and deadly.
When the police yielded my coffin, I was light
As my head when I took aim.'
                              This voice from blight
And hunger died through the black dorm:
There he was, laid out with a drift of Mass cards
At his shrouded feet. Then the firing party's
Volley in the yard. I saw woodworm
In gate posts and door jambs, smelt mildew
From the byre loft where he watched and hid
From fields his draped coffin would raft through.
Unquiet soul, they should have buried you
In the bog where you threw your first grenade,
Where only helicopters and curlews
Make their maimed music, and sphagnum moss
Could teach you its medicinal repose
Until, when the weasel whistles on its tail,
No other weasel will obey its call.

I dreamt and drifted. All seemed to run to waste
As down a swirl of mucky, glittering flood
Strange polyp floated like a huge corrupt
Magnolia bloom, surreal as a shed breast,
My softly awash and blanching self-disgust.
And I cried among night waters, 'I repent
My unweaned life that kept me competent
To sleepwalk with connivance and mistrust.'
Then, like a pistil growing from the polyp,
A lighted candle rose and steadied up
Until the whole bright-masted thing retrieved
A course and the currents it had gone with
Were what it rode and showed. No more adrift,
My feet touched bottom and my heart revived.

Then something round and clear
And mildly turbulent, like a bubbleskin
Or a moon in smoothly rippled lough water
Rose in a cobwebbed space: the molten
Inside-sheen of an instrument
Revolved its polished convexes full
Upon me, so close and brilliant
I seemed to pitch back in a headlong fall.
And then it was the clarity of waking
To sunlight and a bell and gushing taps
In the next cubicle. Still there for the taking!
The old brass trumpet with its valves and stops
I found once in loft thatch, a mystery
I shied from then, for I thought such trove beyond me.

'I hate how quick I was to know my place.
I hate where I was born, hate everything
That made me biddable and unforthcoming,'

I mouthed at my half-composed face
In the shaving mirror, like somebody
Drunk in the bathroom during a party,
Lulled and repelled by his own reflection.
As if the cairnstone could defy the cairn.
As if the eddy could reform the pool.
As if a stone swirled under a cascade,
Eroded and eroding in its bed,
Could grind itself down to a different core.
Then I thought of the tribe whose dances never fail
For they keep dancing till they sight the deer.

New Day, ? "sou-lin spor- (Mari)
"grace" ?
-epiphany of Things - The mug.
cf "Shelf-Life", Pt. I.

X

Morning stir in the hostel. A pot
hooked on forged links. Soot flakes. Plumping water.
The open door brilliant with sunlight.
Hearthsmoke rambling and a thud of earthenware

drumming me back until I saw the mug
beyond my reach on its high shelf, the one
patterned with blue cornflowers, sprig after sprig
repeating round it, as quiet as a milestone . . .

When had it not been there? There was one night
when fit-up actors used it for a prop
and I sat in the dark hall estranged from it
as a couple vowed and called it their loving cup

and held it in our gaze until the curtain
jerked shut with an ordinary noise.
Dipped and glamoured then by this translation,
it was restored to its old haircracked doze

on the mantelpiece, its parchment glazes fast—
as the otter surfaced once with Ronan's psalter
miraculously unharmed, that had been lost
a day and a night under lough water.

And so the saint praised God on the lough shore
for that dazzle of impossibility
I credited again in the sun-filled door,
so absolutely light it could put out fire.

cf. "of the impossible
suddenly" from
1st ed.

cf. Sectoria murder - also sudden
here: moment of repose or
the possibility of the miraculous →
grace / inspiration

XI

As if the prisms of the kaleidoscope
I plunged once in a butt of muddied water
surfaced like a marvellous lightship

and out of its silted crystals a monk's face
that had spoken years ago from behind a grille
spoke again about the need and chance

to salvage everything, to re-envisage
the zenith and glimpsed jewels of any gift
mistakenly abased . . .

What came to nothing could always be replenished.
'Read poems as prayers,' he said, 'and for your penance
translate me something by Juan de la Cruz.'

Returned from Spain to our chapped wilderness,
his consonants aspirate, his forehead shining,
he had made me feel there was nothing to confess.

Now his sandalled passage stirred me on to this:
How well I know that fountain, filling, running,
    although it is the night.

That eternal fountain, hidden away,
I know its haven and its secrecy
    although it is the night.

But not its source because it does not have one,
which is all sources' source and origin
 although it is the night.

No other thing can be so beautiful.
Here the earth and heaven drink their fill
 although it is the night.

So pellucid it never can be muddied,
and I know that all light radiates from it
 although it is the night.

I know no sounding-line can find its bottom,
nobody ford or plumb its deepest fathom
 although it is the night.

And its current so in flood it overspills
to water hell and heaven and all peoples
 although it is the night.

And the current that is generated there,
as far as it wills to, it can flow that far
 although it is the night.

And from these two a third current proceeds
which neither of these two, I know, precedes
 although it is the night.

This eternal fountain hides and splashes
within this living bread that is life to us
 although it is the night.

Hear it calling out to every creature.
And they drink these waters, although it is dark here
    because it is the night.

I am repining for this living fountain.
Within this bread of life I see it plain
    although it is the night.

XII

Like a convalescent, I took the hand
stretched down from the jetty, sensed again
an alien comfort as I stepped on ground

to find the helping hand still gripping mine,
fish-cold and bony, but whether to guide
or to be guided I could not be certain

for the tall man in step at my side
seemed blind, though he walked straight as a rush
upon his ash plant, his eyes fixed straight ahead.

Then I knew him in the flesh
out there on the tarmac among the cars,
wintered hard and sharp as a blackthorn bush.

His voice eddying with the vowels of all rivers
came back to me, though he did not speak yet,
a voice like a prosecutor's or a singer's,

cunning, narcotic, mimic, definite
as a steel nib's downstroke, quick and clean,
and suddenly he hit a litter basket

with his stick, saying, 'Your obligation
is not discharged by any common rite.
What you do you must do on your own.

The main thing is to write
for the joy of it. Cultivate a work-lust
that imagines its haven like your hands at night

dreaming the sun in the sunspot of a breast.
You are fasted now, light-headed, dangerous.
Take off from here. And don't be so earnest,

so ready for the sackcloth and the ashes.
Let go, let fly, forget.
You've listened long enough. Now strike your note.'

It was as if I had stepped free into space
alone with nothing that I had not known
already. Raindrops blew in my face

as I came to and heard the harangue and jeers
going on and on: 'The English language
belongs to us. You are raking at dead fires,

rehearsing the old whinges at your age.
That subject people stuff is a cod's game,
infantile, like this peasant pilgrimage.

You lose more of yourself than you redeem
doing the decent thing. Keep at a tangent.
When they make the circle wide, it's time to swim

out on your own and fill the element
with signatures on your own frequency,
echo-soundings, searches, probes, allurements,

elver-gleams in the dark of the whole sea.'
The shower broke in a cloudburst, the tarmac
fumed and sizzled. As he moved off quickly

the downpour loosed its screens round his straight walk.

From *Sweeney Redivivus*

In the Beech

I was a lookout posted and forgotten.

On one side under me, the concrete road.
On the other, the bullocks' covert,
the breath and plaster of a drinking place
where the school-leaver discovered peace
to touch himself in the reek of churned-up mud.

And the tree itself a strangeness and a comfort,
as much a column as a bole. The very ivy
puzzled its milk-tooth frills and tapers
over the grain: was it bark or masonry?

I watched the red-brick chimney rear
its stamen course by course,
and the steeplejacks up there at their antics
like flies against the mountain.

I felt the tanks' advance beginning
at the cynosure of the growth rings,
then winced at their imperium refreshed
in each powdered bolt mark on the concrete.
And the pilot with his goggles back came in
so low I could see the cockpit rivets.

My hidebound boundary tree. My tree of knowledge.
My thick-tapped, soft-fledged, airy listening post.

The First Kingdom

The royal roads were cow paths.
The queen mother hunkered on a stool
and played the harpstrings of milk
into a wooden pail.
With seasoned sticks the nobles
lorded it over the hindquarters of cattle.

Units of measurement were pondered
by the cartful, barrowful and bucketful.
Time was a backward rote of names and mishaps,
bad harvests, fires, unfair settlements,
deaths in floods, murders and miscarriages.

And if my rights to it all came only
by their acclamation, what was it worth?
I blew hot and blew cold.
They were two-faced and accommodating.
And seed, breed and generation still
they are holding on, every bit
as pious and exacting and demeaned.

The First Flight

It was more sleepwalk than spasm
yet that was a time when the times
were also in spasm—

the ties and the knots running through us
split open
down the lines of the grain.

As I drew close to pebbles and berries,
the smell of wild garlic, relearning
the acoustic of frost

and the meaning of woodnote,
my shadow over the field
was only a spin-off,

my empty place an excuse
for shifts in the camp, old rehearsals
of debts and betrayal.

Singly they came to the tree
with a stone in each pocket
to whistle and bill me back in

and I would collide and cascade
through leaves when they left,
my point of repose knocked askew.

I was mired in attachment
until they began to pronounce me
a feeder off battlefields

so I mastered new rungs of the air
to survey out of reach
their bonfires on hills, their hosting

and fasting, the levies from Scotland
as always, and the people of art
diverting their rhythmical chants

to fend off the onslaught of winds
I would welcome and climb
at the top of my bent.

" negative copy b/w" 'c

Drifting Off

The guttersnipe and the albatross
gliding for days without a single wingbeat
were equally beyond me.

I yearned for the gannet's strike,
the unbegrudging concentration
of the heron.

In the camaraderie of rookeries,
in the spiteful vigilance of colonies
I was at home.

I learned to distrust
the allure of the cuckoo
and the gossip of starlings,

kept faith with doughty bullfinches,
levelled my wit too often
to the small-minded wren

and too often caved in
to the pathos of waterhens
and panicky corncrakes.

I gave much credence to stragglers,
overrated the composure of blackbirds
and the folklore of magpies.

But when goldfinch or kingfisher rent
the veil of the usual,
pinions whispered and braced

as I stooped, unwieldy
and brimming,
my spurs at the ready.

The Cleric

I heard new words prayed at cows
in the byre, found his sign
on the crock and the hidden still,

smelled fumes from his censer
in the first smokes of morning.
Next thing he was making a progress

through gaps, stepping out sites,
sinking his crozier deep
in the fort-hearth.

If he had stuck to his own
cramp-jawed abbesses and intoners
dibbling round the enclosure,

his Latin and blather of love,
his parchments and scheming
in letters shipped over water—

but no, he overbore
with his unctions and orders,
he had to get in on the ground.

History that planted its standards
on his gables and spires
ousted me to the marches

of skulking and whingeing.
Or did I desert?
Give him his due, in the end

he opened my path to a kingdom
of such scope and neuter allegiance
my emptiness reigns at its whim.

The Master

He dwelt in himself
like a rook in an unroofed tower.

To get close I had to maintain
a climb up deserted ramparts
and not flinch, not raise an eye
to search for an eye on the watch
from his coign of seclusion.

Deliberately he would unclasp
his book of withholding
a page at a time and it was nothing
arcane, just the old rules
we all had inscribed on our slates.
Each character blocked on the parchment secure
in its volume and measure.
Each maxim given its space.

Tell the truth. Do not be afraid.
Durable, obstinate notions,
like quarrymen's hammers and wedges proofed
by intransigent service.
Like coping stones where you rest
in the balm of the wellspring.

How flimsy I felt climbing down
the unrailed stairs on the wall,
hearing the purpose and venture
in a wing-flap above me.

The Scribes

I never warmed to them.
If they were excellent they were petulant
and jaggy as the holly tree
they rendered down for ink.
And if I never belonged among them,
they could never deny me my place.

In the hush of the scriptorium
a black pearl kept gathering in them
like the old dry glut inside their quills.
In the margin of texts of praise
they scratched and clawed.
They snarled if the day was dark
or too much chalk had made the vellum bland
or too little left it oily.

Under the rumps of lettering
they herded myopic angers.
Resentment seeded in the uncurling
fernheads of their capitals.

Now and again I started up
miles away and saw in my absence
the sloped cursive of each back and felt them
perfect themselves against me page by page.

Let them remember this not inconsiderable
contribution to their jealous art.

Holly

It rained when it should have snowed.
When we went to gather holly

the ditches were swimming, we were wet
to the knees, our hands were all jags

and water ran up our sleeves.
There should have been berries

but the sprigs we brought into the house
gleamed like smashed bottle-glass.

Now here I am, in a room that is decked
with the red-berried, waxy-leafed stuff,

and I almost forget what it's like
to be wet to the skin or longing for snow.

I reach for a book like a doubter
and want it to flare round my hand,

a black-letter bush, a glittering shield-wall
cutting as holly and ice.

An Artist

I love the thought of his anger.
His obstinacy against the rock, his coercion
of the substance from green apples.

The way he was a dog barking
at the image of himself barking.
And his hatred of his own embrace
of working as the only thing that worked—
the vulgarity of expecting ever
gratitude or admiration, which
would mean a stealing from him.

The way his fortitude held and hardened
because he did what he knew.
His forehead like a hurled *boule*
travelling unpainted space
behind the apple and behind the mountain.

In Illo Tempore

The big missal splayed
and dangled silky ribbons
of emerald and purple and watery white.

Intransitively we would assist,
confess, receive. The verbs
assumed us. We adored.

And we lifted our eyes to the nouns.
Altar stone was dawn and monstrance noon,
the word 'rubric' itself a bloodshot sunset.

Now I live by a famous strand
where seabirds cry in the small hours
like incredible souls

and even the range wall of the promenade
that I press down on for conviction
hardly tempts me to credit it.

On the Road

The road ahead
kept reeling in
at a steady speed,
the verges dripped.

In my hands
like a wrested trophy,
the empty round
of the steering wheel.

The trance of driving
made all roads one:
the seraph-haunted, Tuscan
footpath, the green

oak-alleys of Dordogne
or that track through corn
where the rich young man
asked his question—

*Master, what must I
do to be saved?*
Or the road where the bird
with an earth-red back

and a white and black
tail, like parquet
of flint and jet,
wheeled over me

in visitation.
Sell all you have
and give to the poor.
I was up and away

like a human soul
that plumes from the mouth
in undulant, tenor,
black-letter Latin.

I was one for sorrow,
Noah's dove,
a panicked shadow
crossing the deer path.

If I came to earth
it would be by way of
a small east window
I once squeezed through,

scaling heaven
by superstition,
drunk and happy
on a chapel gable.

I would roost a night
on the slab of exile,
then hide in the cleft
of that churchyard wall

where hand after hand
keeps wearing away

227

at the cold, hard-breasted
votive granite.

And follow me.
I would migrate
through a high cave mouth
into an oaten, sun-warmed cliff,

on down the soft-nubbed,
clay-floored passage,
face-brush, wing-flap,
to the deepest chamber.

There a drinking deer
is cut into rock,
its haunch and neck
rise with the contours,

the incised outline
curves to a strained
expectant muzzle
and a nostril flared

at a dried-up source.
For my book of changes
I would meditate
that stone-faced vigil

until the long dumbfounded
spirit broke cover
to raise a dust
in the font of exhaustion.

FROM

The Haw Lantern

———————————

(1 9 8 7)

For Bernard and Jane McCabe

The riverbed, dried-up, half-full of leaves.

Us, listening to a river in the trees.

Alphabets

A shadow his father makes with joined hands
And thumbs and fingers nibbles on the wall
Like a rabbit's head. He understands
He will understand more when he goes to school.

There he draws smoke with chalk the whole first week,
Then draws the forked stick that they call a Y.
This is writing. A swan's neck and swan's back
Make the 2 he can see now as well as say.

Two rafters and a cross-tie on the slate
Are the letter some call *ah*, some call *ay*.
There are charts, there are headlines, there is a right
Way to hold the pen and a wrong way.

First it is 'copying out', and then 'English'
Marked correct with a little leaning hoe.
Smells of inkwells rise in the classroom hush.
A globe in the window tilts like a coloured O.

II

Declensions sang on air like a *hosanna*
As, column after stratified column,
Book One of *Elementa Latina*,
Marbled and minatory, rose up in him.

For he was fostered next in a stricter school
Named for the patron saint of the oak wood

Where classes switched to the pealing of a bell
And he left the Latin forum for the shade

Of new calligraphy that felt like home.
The letters of this alphabet were trees.
The capitals were orchards in full bloom,
The lines of script like briars coiled in ditches.

Here in her snooded garment and bare feet,
All ringleted in assonance and woodnotes,
The poet's dream stole over him like sunlight
And passed into the tenebrous thickets.

He learns this other writing. He is the scribe
Who drove a team of quills on his white field.
Round his cell door the blackbirds dart and dab.
Then self-denial, fasting, the pure cold.

By rules that hardened the farther they reached north
He bends to his desk and begins again.
Christ's sickle has been in the undergrowth.
The script grows bare and Merovingian.

III

The globe has spun. He stands in a wooden O.
He alludes to Shakespeare. He alludes to Graves.
Time has bulldozed the school and school window.
Balers drop bales like printouts where stooked sheaves

Made lambdas on the stubble once at harvest
And the delta face of each potato pit
Was patted straight and moulded against frost.
All gone, with the omega that kept

Watch above each door, the good-luck horseshoe.
Yet shape-note language, absolute on air
As Constantine's sky-lettered IN HOC SIGNO
Can still command him; or the necromancer

Who would hang from the domed ceiling of his house
A figure of the world with colours in it
So that the figure of the universe
And 'not just single things' would meet his sight

When he walked abroad. As from his small window
The astronaut sees all he has sprung from,
The risen, aqueous, singular, lucent O
Like a magnified and buoyant ovum—

Or like my own wide pre-reflective stare
All agog at the plasterer on his ladder
Skimming our gable and writing our name there
With his trowel point, letter by strange letter.

Terminus

When I hoked there, I would find
An acorn and a rusted bolt.

If I lifted my eyes, a factory chimney
And a dormant mountain.

If I listened, an engine shunting
And a trotting horse.

Is it any wonder when I thought
I would have second thoughts?

When they spoke of the prudent squirrel's hoard
It shone like gifts at a nativity.

When they spoke of the mammon of iniquity
The coins in my pockets reddened like stove-lids.

I was the march drain and the march drain's banks
Suffering the limit of each claim.

Two buckets were easier carried than one.
I grew up in between.

My left hand placed the standard iron weight.
My right tilted a last grain in the balance.

Baronies, parishes met where I was born.
When I stood on the central stepping stone

I was the last earl on horseback in midstream
Still parleying, in earshot of his peers.

From the Frontier of Writing

The tightness and the nilness round that space
when the car stops in the road, the troops inspect
its make and number and, as one bends his face

towards your window, you catch sight of more
on a hill beyond, eyeing with intent
down cradled guns that hold you under cover

and everything is pure interrogation
until a rifle motions and you move
with guarded unconcerned acceleration—

a little emptier, a little spent
as always by that quiver in the self,
subjugated, yes, and obedient.

So you drive on to the frontier of writing
where it happens again. The guns on tripods;
the sergeant with his on-off mike repeating

data about you, waiting for the squawk
of clearance; the marksman training down
out of the sun upon you like a hawk.

And suddenly you're through, arraigned yet freed,
as if you'd passed from behind a waterfall
on the black current of a tarmac road

past armour-plated vehicles, out between
the posted soldiers flowing and receding
like tree shadows into the polished windscreen.

Situation? or identity?
analogy
Persuasive? or end?
equipoise

The Haw Lantern

The wintry haw is burning out of season,
crab of the thorn, a small light for small people,
wanting no more from them but that they keep
the wick of self-respect from dying out,
not having to blind them with illumination.

But sometimes when your breath plumes in the frost
it takes the roaming shape of Diogenes
with his lantern, seeking one just man;
so you end up scrutinized from behind the haw
he holds up at eye-level on its twig,
and you flinch before its bonded pith and stone,
its blood-prick that you wish would test and clear you,
its pecked-at ripeness that scans you, then moves on.

From the Republic of Conscience

What is it like?
"dual citizenship"
means?

I

When I landed in the republic of conscience
it was so noiseless when the engines stopped
I could hear a curlew high above the runway.

At immigration, the clerk was an old man
who produced a wallet from his homespun coat
and showed me a photograph of my grandfather.

The woman in customs asked me to declare
the words of our traditional cures and charms
to heal dumbness and avert the evil eye.

No porters. No interpreter. No taxi.
You carried your own burden and very soon
your symptoms of creeping privilege disappeared.

II

Fog is a dreaded omen there but lightning
spells universal good and parents hang
swaddled infants in trees during thunderstorms.

Salt is their precious mineral. And seashells
are held to the ear during births and funerals.
The base of all inks and pigments is seawater.

Their sacred symbol is a stylized boat.
The sail is an ear, the mast a sloping pen,
The hull a mouth-shape, the keel an open eye.

At their inauguration, public leaders
must swear to uphold unwritten law and weep
to atone for their presumption to hold office—

and to affirm their faith that all life sprang
from salt in tears which the sky-god wept
after he dreamt his solitude was endless.

III

I came back from that frugal republic
with my two arms the one length, the customs woman
having insisted my allowance was myself.

The old man rose and gazed into my face
and said that was official recognition
that I was now a dual citizen.

He therefore desired me when I got home
to consider myself a representative
and to speak on their behalf in my own tongue.

Their embassies, he said, were everywhere
but operated independently
and no ambassador would ever be relieved.

Hailstones

My cheek was hit and hit:
sudden hailstones
pelted and bounced on the road.

When it cleared again
something whipped and knowledgeable
had withdrawn

and left me there with my chances.
I made a small hard ball
of burning water running from my hand

just as I make this now
out of the melt of the real thing
smarting into its absence.

II

To be reckoned with, all the same,
those brats of showers.
The way they refused permission,

rattling the classroom window
like a ruler across the knuckles,
the way they were perfect first

and then in no time dirty slush.
Thomas Traherne had his orient wheat
for proof and wonder

but for us, it was the sting of hailstones
and the unstingable hands of Eddie Diamond
foraging in the nettles.

III

Nipple and hive, bite-lumps,
small acorns of the almost pleasurable
intimated and disallowed

when the shower ended
and everything said *wait.*
For what? For forty years

to say there, there you had
the truest foretaste of your aftermath—
in that dilation

when the light opened in silence
and a car with wipers going still
laid perfect tracks in the slush.

The Stone Verdict

When he stands in the judgement place
With his stick in his hand and the broad hat
Still on his head, maimed by self-doubt
And an old disdain of sweet talk and excuses,
It will be no justice if the sentence is blabbed out.
He will expect more than words in the ultimate court
He relied on through a lifetime's speechlessness.

Let it be like the judgement of Hermes,
God of the stone heap, where the stones were verdicts
Cast solidly at his feet, piling up around him
Until he stood waist-deep in the cairn
Of his apotheosis: maybe a gate-pillar
Or a tumbled wallstead where hogweed earths the silence
Somebody will break at last to say, 'Here
His spirit lingers,' and will have said too much.

The Spoonbait

So a new similitude is given us
And we say: The soul may be compared

Unto a spoonbait that a child discovers
Beneath the sliding lid of a pencil case,

Glimpsed once and imagined for a lifetime
Risen and free and spooling out of nowhere—

A shooting star going back up the darkness.
It flees him and it burns him all at once

Like the single drop that Dives implored
Falling and falling into a great gulf.

Then exit, the polished helmet of a hero
Laid out amidships above scudding water.

Exit, alternatively, a toy of light
Reeled through him upstream, snagging on nothing.

Clearances

In Memoriam M.K.H., 1911–1984

She taught me what her uncle once taught her:
How easily the biggest coal block split
If you got the grain and hammer angled right.

The sound of that relaxed alluring blow,
Its co-opted and obliterated echo,
Taught me to hit, taught me to loosen,

Taught me between the hammer and the block
To face the music/Teach me now to listen,
To strike it rich behind the linear black.

1

A cobble thrown a hundred years ago
Keeps coming at me, the first stone
Aimed at a great-grandmother's turncoat brow.
The pony jerks and the riot's on.
She's crouched low in the trap
Running the gauntlet that first Sunday
Down the brae to Mass at a panicked gallop.
He whips on through the town to cries of 'Lundy!'

Call her 'The Convert'. 'The Exogamous Bride'.
Anyhow, it is a genre piece
Inherited on my mother's side
And mine to dispose with now she's gone.
Instead of silver and Victorian lace,
The exonerating, exonerated stone.

246

2

Polished linoleum shone there. Brass taps shone.
The china cups were very white and big—
An unchipped set with sugar bowl and jug.
The kettle whistled. Sandwich and tea scone
Were present and correct. In case it run,
The butter must be kept out of the sun.
And don't be dropping crumbs. Don't tilt your chair.
Don't reach. Don't point. Don't make noise when you stir.

It is Number 5, New Row, Land of the Dead,
Where grandfather is rising from his place
With spectacles pushed back on a clean bald head
To welcome a bewildered homing daughter
Before she even knocks. 'What's this? What's this?'
And they sit down in the shining room together.

Then ? ?
Now ! ?
Relationship !

3

When all the others were away at Mass
I was all hers as we peeled potatoes.
They broke the silence, let fall one by one
Like solder weeping off the soldering iron:
Cold comforts set between us, things to share
Gleaming in a bucket of clean water.
And again let fall. Little pleasant splashes
From each other's work would bring us to our senses.

So while the parish priest at her bedside
Went hammer and tongs at the prayers for the dying
And some were responding and some crying
I remembered her head bent towards my head,
Her breath in mine, our fluent dipping knives—
Never closer the whole rest of our lives.

Then / Now ?
Weight of silence

248

4

Fear of affectation made her affect
Inadequacy whenever it came to
Pronouncing words 'beyond her'. *Bertold Brek.*
She'd manage something hampered and askew
Every time, as if she might betray
The hampered and inadequate by too
Well-adjusted a vocabulary.
With more challenge than pride, she'd tell me, 'You
Know all them things.' So I governed my tongue
In front of her, a genuinely well-
Adjusted adequate betrayal
Of what I knew better. I'd *naw* and *aye*
And decently relapse into the wrong
Grammar which kept us allied and at bay.

249

5

The cool that came off sheets just off the line
Made me think the damp must still be in them
But when I took my corners of the linen
And pulled against her, first straight down the hem
And then diagonally, then flapped and shook
The fabric like a sail in a cross-wind,
They made a dried-out undulating thwack.
So we'd stretch and fold and end up hand to hand
For a split second as if nothing had happened
For nothing had that had not always happened
Beforehand, day by day, just touch and go,
Coming close again by holding back
In moves where I was x and she was o
Inscribed in sheets she'd sewn from ripped-out flour sacks.

6

In the first flush of the Easter holidays
The ceremonies during Holy Week
Were highpoints of our *Sons and Lovers* phase.
The midnight fire. The paschal candlestick.
Elbow to elbow, glad to be kneeling next
To each other up there near the front
Of the packed church, we would follow the text
And rubrics for the blessing of the font.
As the hind longs for the streams, so my soul . . .
Dippings. Towellings. The water breathed on.
The water mixed with chrism and with oil.
Cruet tinkle. Formal incensation
And the psalmist's outcry taken up with pride:
Day and night my tears have been my bread.

Easter | Passover

Time?

Ps 42 . blessing of the fount en
Holy Saturday

7

In the last minutes he said more to her
Almost than in all their life together.
'You'll be in New Row on Monday night
And I'll come up for you and you'll be glad
When I walk in the door . . . Isn't that right?'
His head was bent down to her propped-up head.
She could not hear but we were overjoyed.
He called her good and girl. Then she was dead,
The searching for a pulsebeat was abandoned
And we all knew one thing by being there.
The space we stood around had been emptied
Into us to keep, it penetrated
Clearances that suddenly stood open.
High cries were felled and a pure change happened.

8

I thought of walking round and round a space
Utterly empty, utterly a source
Where the decked chestnut tree had lost its place
In our front hedge above the wallflowers.
The white chips jumped and jumped and skited high.
I heard the hatchet's differentiated
Accurate cut, the crack, the sigh
And collapse of what luxuriated
Through the shocked tips and wreckage of it all.
Deep-planted and long gone, my coeval
Chestnut from a jam jar in a hole,
Its heft and hush become a bright nowhere,
A soul ramifying and forever
Silent, beyond silence listened for.

The Milk Factory

Scuts of froth swirled from the discharge pipe.
We halted on the other bank and watched
A milky water run from the pierced side
Of milk itself, the crock of its substance spilt
Across white limbo floors where shift-workers
Waded round the clock, and the factory
Kept its distance like a bright-decked star-ship.

There we go, soft-eyed calves of the dew,
Astonished and assumed into fluorescence.

The Wishing Tree

I thought of her as the wishing tree that died
And saw it lifted, root and branch, to heaven,
Trailing a shower of all that had been driven

Need by need by need into its hale
Sap-wood and bark: coin and pin and nail
Came streaming from it like a comet-tail

New-minted and dissolved. I had a vision
Of an airy branch-head rising through damp cloud,
Of turned-up faces where the tree had stood.

Wolfe Tone

Light as a skiff, manoeuvrable
yet outmanoeuvred,

I affected epaulettes and a cockade,
wrote a style well-bred and impervious

to the solidarity I angled for,
and played the ancient Roman with a razor.

I was the shouldered oar that ended up
far from the brine and whiff of venture,

like a scratching-post or a crossroads flagpole,
out of my element among small farmers—

I who once wakened to the shouts of men
rising from the bottom of the sea,

men in their shirts mounting through deep water
when the Atlantic stove our cabin's dead lights in

and the big fleet split and Ireland dwindled
as we ran before the gale under bare poles.

Then + now
old + new

colonial + post-colonial
cf " Wherever you say — "
91

From the Canton of Expectation

I   of wash

cf "1919"

We lived deep in a land of optative moods,
under high, banked clouds of resignation.
A rustle of loss in the phrase *Not in our lifetime*,
the broken nerve when we prayed *Vouchsafe* or *Deign*,
were creditable, sufficient to the day.

Once a year we gathered in a field
of dance platforms and tents where children sang
songs they had learned by rote in the old language.
An auctioneer who had fought in the brotherhood
enumerated the humiliations
we always took for granted, but not even he
considered this, I think, a call to action.
Iron-mouthed loudspeakers shook the air
yet nobody felt blamed. He had confirmed us.
When our rebel anthem played the meeting shut
we turned for home and the usual harassment
by militiamen on overtime at roadblocks.

II

And next thing, suddenly, this change of mood.
Books open in the newly wired kitchens.
Young heads that might have dozed a life away
against the flanks of milking cows were busy
paving and pencilling their first causeways
across the prescribed texts. The paving stones
of quadrangles came next and a grammar
of imperatives, the new age of demands.

257

They would banish the conditional for ever,
this generation born impervious to
the triumph in our cries of *de profundis*.
Our faith in winning by enduring most
they made anathema, intelligences
brightened and unmannerly as crowbars.

III

What looks the strongest has outlived its term.
The future lies with what's affirmed from under.
These things that corroborated us when we dwelt
under the aegis of our stealthy patron,
the guardian angel of passivity,
now sink a fang of menace in my shoulder.
I repeat the word 'stricken' to myself
and stand bareheaded under the banked clouds
edged more and more with brassy thunderlight.
I yearn for hammerblows on clinkered planks,
the uncompromised report of driven thole-pins,
to know there is one among us who never swerved
from all his instincts told him was right action,
who stood his ground in the indicative,
whose boat will lift when the cloudburst happens.

The Mud Vision

Statues with exposed hearts and barbed-wire crowns
Still stood in alcoves, hares flitted beneath
The dozing bellies of jets, our menu-writers
And punks with aerosol sprays held their own
With the best of them. Satellite link-ups
Wafted over us the blessings of popes, heliports
Maintained a charmed circle for idols on tour
And casualties on their stretchers. We sleepwalked
The line between panic and formulae, screentested
Our first native models and the last of the mummers,
Watching ourselves at a distance, advantaged
And airy as a man on a springboard
Who keeps limbering up because the man cannot dive.

And then in the foggy midlands it appeared,
Our mud vision, as if a rose window of mud
Had invented itself out of the glittery damp,
A gossamer wheel, concentric with its own hub
Of nebulous dirt, sullied yet lucent.
We had heard of the sun standing still and the sun
That changed colour, but we were vouchsafed
Original clay, transfigured and spinning.
And then the sunsets ran murky, the wiper
Could never entirely clean off the windscreen,
Reservoirs tasted of silt, a light fuzz
Accrued in the hair and the eyebrows, and some
Took to wearing a smudge on their foreheads
To be prepared for whatever. Vigils
Began to be kept around puddled gaps,

On altars bulrushes ousted the lilies
And a rota of invalids came and went
On beds they could lease placed in range of the shower.

A generation who had seen a sign!
Those nights when we stood in an umber dew and smelled
Mould in the verbena, or woke to a light
Furrow-breath on the pillow, when the talk
Was all about who had seen it and our fear
Was touched with a secret pride, only ourselves
Could be adequate then to our lives. When the rainbow
Curved flood-brown and ran like a water-rat's back
So that drivers on the hard shoulder switched off to watch,
We wished it away, and yet we presumed it a test
That would prove us beyond expectation.

We lived, of course, to learn the folly of that.
One day it was gone and the east gable
Where its trembling corolla had balanced
Was starkly a ruin again, with dandelions
Blowing high up on the ledges, and moss
That slumbered on through its increase. As cameras raked
The site from every angle, experts
Began their *post factum* jabber and all of us
Crowded in tight for the big explanations.
Just like that, we forgot that the vision was ours,
Our one chance to know the incomparable
And dive to a future. What might have been origin
We dissipated in news. The clarified place
Had retrieved neither us nor itself—except
You could say we survived. So say that, and watch us
Who had our chance to be mud-men, convinced and
        estranged,
Figure in our own eyes for the eyes of the world.

The Disappearing Island

Once we presumed to found ourselves for good
Between its blue hills and those sandless shores
Where we spent our desperate night in prayer and vigil,

Once we had gathered driftwood, made a hearth
And hung our cauldron like a firmament,
The island broke beneath us like a wave.

The land sustaining us seemed to hold firm
Only when we embraced it in extremis.
All I believe that happened there was vision.

Notes

The pieces from *Stations* included here were first printed in a pamphlet in Belfast (Ulsterman Publications, 1975); and the extracts from *Sweeney Astray* are based upon Irish originals in *Buile Suibhne*. Sweeney's voice is also present, displaced out of its medieval context, in 'Sweeney Redivivus'.

'Station Island' is set upon an island of that name in Lough Derg in County Donegal. For centuries it has been the site of a pilgrimage which involves fasting, praying, and going barefoot around the 'beds'—stone circles believed to be the remaining foundations of early monastic buildings. Each unit of these penitential exercises is called a 'station'. William Carleton, who figures in Section II, published a famous account of his experiences on the island in *Traits and Stories of the Irish Peasantry* (1830–33). The poem by Saint John of the Cross translated in Section XI is 'Cantar del alma que se huelga de conoscar a Dios por fe'. (Further annotations to this title poem and to some other poems in the volume are available in *Station Island*.)

S.H.

Index of Titles

Index of First Lines